Thyme & The River Too

THYME & THE RIVER TOO

Brunches, Lunches, Picnics, Dinners & Desserts
from the Northwest's Steamboat Inn

by Sharon Van Loan and Patricia Lee
with Trey Combs

GRAPHIC ARTS CENTER PUBLISHING™

International Standard Book Number 1-55868-155-8
Library of Congress Catalog Card Number 93-78466
©MCMXCIII Graphic Arts Center Publishing Company
P.O. Box 10306 • Portland, Oregon 97210 • 503/226-2402
All rights reserved. No part of this book may be reproduced
by any means without written permission of the publisher.
"Steelhead Flies of the North Umpqua," ©MCMXCI by Trey Combs.
Adapted with permission from chapters 9 and 38, *Steelhead Fly Fishing*,
Lyons & Burford, Publishers, New York
Scenic Photography ©MCMXCIII Dan Callaghan
Drawings ©MCMXCIII David Hall
Food Photography ©MCMXCIII John Rizzo
Food Stylist • Lori McKean
Photographer's Assistant • Matt Cooper
President • Charles M. Hopkins
Editor-in-Chief • Douglas A. Pfeiffer
Managing Editor • Jean Andrews
Production Manager • Richard L. Owsiany
Designer • Becky Gyes
Typographer • Harrison Typesetting, Inc.
Printer • Dynagraphics, Inc.
Bindery • Lincoln & Allen
Steamboat Inn • Steamboat, Oregon 97447-9703 • 503/498-2411
Printed in the United States of America

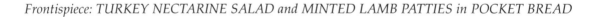

Frontispiece: TURKEY NECTARINE SALAD and MINTED LAMB PATTIES in POCKET BREAD

Contents

To our staff,
whose good humor and energies have contributed
not only to this book but also to the success of the Inn.

SHARON VAN LOAN and PATRICIA LEE

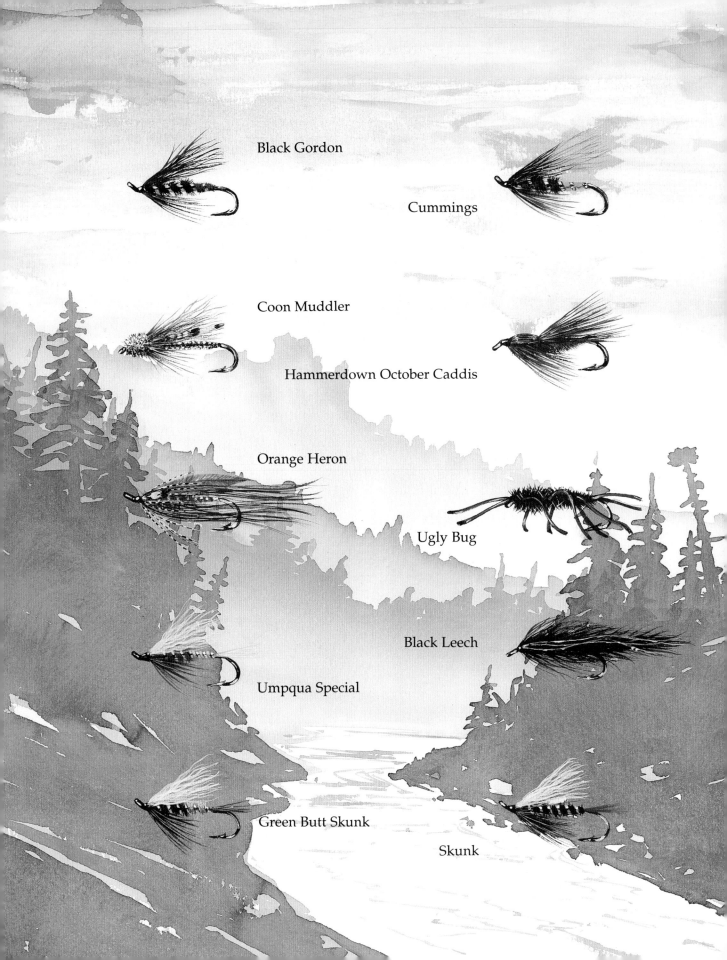

Black Gordon

Cummings

Coon Muddler

Hammerdown October Caddis

Orange Heron

Ugly Bug

Black Leech

Umpqua Special

Green Butt Skunk

Skunk

Steelhead Flies of the North Umpqua

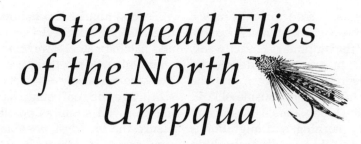

by Trey Combs

On a fog-grey high-tide dawn in early April, the first of the North Umpqua's spring-run steelhead come in from the ocean. As they pass between North Spit, the cape of great white sand dunes, and the lighthouse signaling the south entrance of Winchester Bay, their travel is unhurried, still somewhat random. Unless feeding, they cover a mile in an hour swimming a meter below the surface.

The shoreline becomes a new and constant bearing. Brackish estuary channels, skeins of smells vaguely familiar to the steelhead, appear and disappear under the opposing forces of gravitational action, the tides of the sea, and the gradient of the river. Some few molecules of river, imprinted on their subconscious years before, fix their attention and hold them during the ebbing tide. Several steelhead, nervous and tentative, break from the group and ghost-in on the evening's flood tide. They begin tracking their origins, deliberation becoming a compulsion that carries them past the bridge at Reedsport and almost beyond the reach of the tides. By nightfall they have taken up stations near the beach. They rock almost imperceptibly with the faint currents and pass their first night as adult steelhead in the Umpqua River.

Movement upriver is sporadic and highly individual. Three miles per day is a good average, the greater part taken in the afternoon, when the sun has raised the river's temperature a few degrees. The steelhead are frequently seduced by the strange smells of tributary creeks, and a single fish may stop to breathe in their heady turbulence for days.

The steelhead are so immature sexually that they will not spawn for ten months. About three of every four fish have spent two years in the ocean, one in four but a single year. As a race, they average seven pounds. The rare steelhead—two or three in every hundred—has stayed out for three years. These are usually males, and they have been known to reach twenty pounds.

The temperature of the Umpqua rises each week, ten degrees in a single month, twenty degrees by late spring, thirty degrees by summer, and the steelhead of May and June are more businesslike in their drive for spawning headwaters. The river is at its coolest in the early morning, and migration is best resumed then. The creeks can still be refreshing layovers, but steelhead tarrying too long in August will be trapped, the water reaching eighty degrees. Ultimately the creeks, too, will become lethally warm, and the steelhead will perish.

Halfway through their journey, the river splits. Unerringly, the steelhead choose the branch that leads north; two days later they reach Winchester Dam on the North Umpqua. Six weeks have passed since they crossed the tidal bar at Winchester Bay.

At the dam is a fish ladder, the first serious impediment to upstream progress, a temporary source of intimidation. Once they enter, however, they transit the ladder quickly.

An employee of the Oregon Department of Fish and Game sits in a viewing chamber and peers into the fish ladder through a plexiglas window. He works a single eight-hour shift—usually from four in the morning until noon—and records each steelhead that passes. The afternoon-to-evening shift, only occasionally completed, provides a necessary frame of reference. All information is fed into a computer. Few, if any, steelhead pass up the ladder at night, and some extrapolation is necessary, for not every fish has been observed, but the overall count is accurate.

As the count proceeds, the steelhead are easily divided into three groups. At least three of every four are fin-clipped hatchery stock, the fleshy little caudal peduncle, the fin behind the dorsal fin, having been completely removed by hatchery personnel just before release. Most of the remaining steelhead are wild-born, native North Umpqua stock. Several winter-run steelhead may appear. These are dark, highly colored, and ready to spawn.

Within a week, the steelhead have entered the bedrock canyon water for which the North Umpqua is famous, and reached Rock Creek, the first of several major spawning tributaries.

Several hundred feet above the mouth of Rock Creek is the Rock Creek Hatchery, where both wild and hatchery stocks are temporarily blocked by a weir. Only wild steelhead are used for brood stock. They are purposely not selected for any particular size or age, the goal being a hatchery plant as much like the wild strain as possible. Furthermore, to assure the broadest possible run timing, brood stock are secured throughout the many weeks covering the main body of the run.

As the wild steelhead arrive, they are held in a concrete pen to grow to sexual maturity until they are ready to be spawned in December or January. The 300 thousand eggs gathered will result, one year later, in a plant of approximately 170 thousand smolts, five or six to the pound, each about eight inches long. Mortality is extremely high—only five percent or fewer survive to return as adults. In the meantime, hundreds of native steelhead proceed up Rock Creek to spawn naturally.

The steelhead that have continued up the North Umpqua—including many born and reared in the Rock Creek Hatchery—have already entered the thirty-four-mile-long fly-fishing-only section. Most are nearing their final destination, the Steamboat Creek, eighteen river miles above Rock Creek, the most important spawning tributary for native steelhead in the entire North Umpqua system. It has taken them two months to travel the 125 miles from the coast. They remain chrome-bright and magnificently strong. The steelhead will not immediately enter their home stream, preferring instead to concentrate in the holding water immediately below the confluence.

These are the pools of North Umpqua legend, a series of ledge-rock channels, rapids, riffles, and glides, each with a name, a special character, and a history. They are the most celebrated waters in all of steelhead fly fishing.

No less storied are the first anglers who came to the North Umpqua to explore these pools and to build a fly fishing tradition now hallowed here as on no other western river. This roll call from the river's past includes Major Jordan Lawrence Mott, Zane Grey, Fred Burnham, Joe DeBernardi, Clarence Gordon, Ward Cummings, Ray Bergman, Clark Van Fleet, and Claude Krieder. These men lived the river, wrote about their experiences and, by cross pollinating flies brought from other rivers and fisheries, birthed steelhead dressings uniquely North Umpqua in color and spirit. The generations of fly fishers who followed, those who annually made the pilgrimage to Steamboat to walk the trails, to recite the names of pools, and to tell stories of Gordon and Grey, wrote their own histories and added to the river's growing mystique. I think of Frank Moore, Ernest Schweibert, Jack Hemingway, Stan Knouse, Ken Anderson, and Dan Callaghan. If the river at times seems heartless to a romantic, it is endlessly fascinating to the professional fly fishers, the technocrats whose wisdom often transcends genteel bows to fly tying traditions, and who hunt for steelhead with flies as rag-tag ugly as they are effective. These pragmatic anglers, too, love the river well, meld their lives to its ways, and regularly hook fish when others cannot. They see the river as a litmus test for fly fishing abilities, yet know better than most the folly of swaggering claims of expertise. The very best of them share their hard-won understandings, a giving that promotes the kind of protective attitude the fly fishing public reserves for a few great rivers. Many anglers are in this group, but I think first of Joe Howell, Dennis Black, Dave Hall, and Brad Jackson.

The steelhead patterns associated with this river and the gossip that surrounds their invention, from the Umpqua Special to the Marabou Leech, have become the most tangible way to count the years and to recall the exploits of the great North Umpqua fly fishers, past and present. The story has no documented beginning, but could start with the fly that bears the river's name, the Umpqua Special.

During several summers that came to be celebrated forever in valley legend, Zane Grey, his son Romer, and an entourage of secretaries, cooks, packers, and guides descended upon the North Umpqua. Grey fished American and English wet flies and a handful of Rogue River patterns tied for him by Joe Wharton, a sporting goods store owner from Grants Pass. He especially favored the hairwing Coachman and Parmachene Belle, and followed these choices with the Turkey and Red and the Turkey and Gold. Grey asked that Wharton add a brown bucktail wing to an orange demon-type fly

he had first fished in New Zealand, and the Golden Demon filled out his short list. By the late 1930s he was fishing the Umpqua Special, but history is less certain of his input to the development of the fly.

The Umpqua Special's blood lines are evident: A Parmachene Beau and Parmachene Belle, a hairwing cross that took place first on the Rogue River. The Rogue River Special—"special" for the jungle cock cheeks—certainly bears a close resemblance. Rumor suggests that when Zane Grey came to the Umpqua and hired Joe DeBernardi to guide him for steelhead, the Umpqua Special developed out of their close association.

(Because of the difficulty—and expense—of obtaining genuine jungle cock, today's Umpqua Special is usually tied as described.)

Umpqua Special

Tail: White bucktail.
Body: Rear, one-third yellow wool; front, two-thirds red wool. Rib entire body with silver tinsel.

Wing: White bucktail. Shoulder with a few strands of red bucktail on each side.
Hackle: Brown, tied in over wing.

Clarence Gordon permeates nearly every seam of North Umpqua lore. He first visited the river in 1929 to fly fish for its steelhead and soon became obsessed with the waters below Steamboat Creek. After obtaining a lease from the Forest Service, he built a lodge on the south side of the river in 1934. Gordon, the archetypal fly fisher, acted as host, guide, and fly tier. Guests arrived from all over the world. No other river at the time so strongly defined steelhead fly fishing.

At Gordon's invitation, Ray Bergman, the fishing editor of *Outdoor Life*, came to Steamboat and wrote about his experiences in *Trout* (Knopf, 1938).

Clark C. Van Fleet frequently visited the river, and in his book, *Steelhead to a Fly* (Atlantic, Little Brown, 1951), he said, "You will find in Clarence Gordon an expert on the ways of the fish in these waters, casting a beautiful fly himself and fully acquainted with all the hot spots."

Claude Krieder found the North Umpqua a very tough proposition, and wrote in the book, *Steelhead*

(G. P. Putnam's Sons, 1948), "I sought the famous Mott Pool and the Kitchen Pool, waters in which many tremendous steelhead had been taken over the years by the great among the Umpqua specialists. And none of them yielded a single strike."

Clarence Gordon soon added his own name to the list of North Umpqua steelhead dressings. None survived time better than the Black Gordon, and it remains one of the river's few "standards."

Black Gordon

Body: Rear, one-third red yarn; front, two-thirds black yarn. Rib body with narrow oval gold tinsel.

Hackle: Black.
Wing: Black or very dark brown bucktail.

Two lesser-known Gordon patterns, the Grey Gordon and the Orange Gordon, are quite effective.

Grey Gordon

Body: Black dubbing with a silver tinsel rib.
Hackle: Guinea.

Wing: Grey squirrel.
Tail: Lady Amherst tippet.

Orange Gordon

Tail: Bronze mallard.
Body: Orange wool with a gold tinsel rib.

Hackle: Brown.
Wing: Bronze mallard. (Brown bucktail was later substituted.)

Two caddis species of the genus *Dicosmoecus* are found on the North Umpqua: the grey sedge, commonly seen in late spring and summer; and the orange fall caddis, the famous "October Caddis," found in late summer and fall. Each is about two inches long. I believe Gordon was inspired by both caddis when he developed these patterns.

Ward Cummings, a fishing buddy of Gordon's, helped develop an alternate to the Black Gordon. He told me of its invention this way: "The fly was given birth one night through the brainstorm of two fly addicts and a quart of Ballantine Scotch." Of course, Clarence Gordon was the other "fly addict."

Cummings

Body: Rear, one-third yellow floss; front, two-thirds claret or wine wool, ribbed with silver tinsel.

Hackle: Wine or claret.
Wing: Natural brown bucktail.
Tail: None.

Clarence Gordon closed the North Umpqua Lodge from 1952 to 1955 when the Toketee Dam upriver so silted the North Umpqua that fishing was impossible. He later sold the lodge to the Forest Service, and opened up the Steamboat Store on the north bank. Though first built to cater to construction crews, Gordon added a kitchen and dining facilities. When he and his wife, Delia, retired, they sold the Steamboat Store to Frank and Jeanne Moore. Frank, a well-known steelhead guide and Roseburg restauranteur, soon built guest cabins, and renamed the business Steamboat Inn.

Frank Moore told me the story of the Skunk, the most famous pattern in all of steelhead fly fishing. "Mildred Krogel was from Roseburg. She first tied the pattern for her husband, Lawrence, and her kids. It was in the later 1930s or early 1940s that she was tying it. They used to come up here and stay at Canton Creek Campground the entire summer. They would have a race each morning to see who would get the 'pool of the year.' Sometimes this was Station, other times Kitchen, and so on."

The Skunk remains Moore's favorite steelhead fly, even after Dan Callaghan, his fishing companion and consummate photographer of the river, added a hot green butt to the fly. Today, fly fishers call upon the magic powers of the Green Butt Skunk more than any other dressing in the sport.

Skunk

Body: Black chenille, or black dubbing ribbed with silver tinsel.

Hackle: Black.
Wing: White bucktail.
Tail: Red hackle fibers.

Joe and Bonnie Howell own the Blue Heron Fly Shop in Idleyld Park. Though in business only since the early 1980s, the shop has become an institution. Joe is known nationally as a premier guide with an intuitive understanding of the North Umpqua and its steelhead. When our schedules permit, we fish together and spend hours talking about steelhead and the fly patterns we think best move them. This often takes the form of, "If you only had three patterns . . ." Joe's choices are traditional and dark: the Muddler, the Skunk, the Black Gordon. But, of course, he cannot leave it at that. For soft water, dead drifts, late summer season, and the steelhead of winter, he has developed four beautiful spey-type flies: the Orange Heron 1, Orange Heron 2, Silver Streak, and Gold Streak.

Orange Heron 1

Tag: Flat silver tinsel.
Body: Rear half, fluorescent orange floss; front half hot orange seal fur. Rib entire body with fine oval gold tinsel.
Cheeks: Jungle cock.

Spey hackle: Extra-wide black saddle hackle. (Strip one side first.)
Wing: Four matching hackle tips dyed fluorescent orange.
Throat: Two turns of teal (strip feather on one side first).

Orange Heron 2

Tag and Body: Identical to Orange Heron 1.
Body Hackle: Natural heron or substitute.

Throat: Teal, two turns.
Wing: Matching sections of peacock secondary wing quills.

Silver Streak

Body: Flat silver tinsel ribbed with oval gold tinsel; palmered with long heron hackle.

Throat: Guinea dyed blue.
Wing: Bronze mallard.
Tag: Flat silver tinsel.

Gold Streak

Tag: Flat gold tinsel.
Body: Rear half, orange floss; front half, hot orange seal fur. Rib body with narrow oval gold tinsel.

Body hackle: Heron, natural.
Throat: Guinea, dyed orange.
Wing: Bronze mallard.

One morning, Joe and I fished Famous Pool, a punchbowl of ledge rock with steelhead holding in brilliantly clear water of very moderate current. On such placid water he fishes dry flies, casting upstream for drag-free floats. He looks for virgin fish (steelhead that have not been cast over that day), and he favors the cooler waters of late summer and fall. He uses three patterns: the Muddler, the Royal Wulff, and the high floating MacIntosh—the latter better known as an Atlantic salmon dry.

When skating dries, Joe fishes two patterns of his own design, the Golden Stone and the Orange Scooter. Both are variations of the Muddler. In that context, he calls his "standard" Muddler a Coon Muddler. Because of the difficulty and expense in obtaining oak turkey when he ties commercially for his shop, he has taken to substituting matching slips of white-tipped wood duck for the underwing and raccoon for the overwing. He feels this variation is at least as effective as the original.

Orange Scooter

Tail: Orange Krystal Flash.
Body: Fluorescent orange wool, thin.

Wing: Orange Krystal Flash; black bucktail over.
Head: Spun deer body hair, dyed black.

The Orange Scooter meets Joe's need for a high-visibility silhouette pattern that can be waked on a floating line, or fished subsurface on the swing with a sink-tip line.

Golden Stone

Body: Palmered gold wool, furnace saddle.
Wing: Natural elk, tan-colored. Tie in brown saddle hackle at the head.

Head: Deer body hair dyed gold, spun and clipped to shape. Palmer head with brown saddle.
Tail: Moose.

The golden stone (*Acroneuria californica*) is abundant on the North Umpqua in June, with sporadic hatches taking place through July and August. Joe's Golden Stone matches this hatch. Though dressed full, the fly rides low, its large head setting up a sizable wake on the swing. This is an excellent floater, especially for midsummer fishing on the pools below Steamboat.

For June and much of July, the steelhead moving up the North Umpqua are plainly in a hurry. I have watched them, an hour after first light, move through a pool in a few minutes, oblivious to any fly offered. They are more responsive near their destinations, holding stations for longer periods of time.

The North Umpqua at Steamboat that is fifty degrees the first of June will top sixty degrees by the end of July, as the main stem downriver reaches eighty degrees. Some combination of time in the river and water at least twenty degrees warmer than when they entered makes the fish dour and hard to move from deep lies. Except for first and last light, casting over steelhead using a greased-line method is frustrating.

Joe says then you often must "hit a steelhead on the head" with a small fly to get it to take. At the same time, repeated mends while using a small fly are much less likely to put a steelhead off. Because a large 3/0 or even 4/0 silhouette pattern is certain to cause some sort of response from a steelhead, Joe leaves this approach for last.

Several approaches, all involving going down to the fish, can then be used. The heavily weighted flies generally fall into two categories, black leeches and dark nymphs as complicated as Kaufmann's Stone or as simple as the Montana Nymph and any black Girdle-Bug-type rubber-leg nymph.

"Black Leech" is more generic than specific. Any fly with black marabou tied on a heavily weighted hook qualifies. Joe alternately calls the fly Ugly Bug, Thump Bug, and Beaded Wonder. Everyone seems to apologize for its use; no one questions its effectiveness. The following is a typical example.

Black Leech

Tail: Black marabou, short.
Body: Black chenille ribbed with silver tinsel; palmer with webby black hackle.

Hackle: Black, long and webby.
Head: Flame single strand floss.

A variation of the black maribou leech in popular demand involves the use of two hooks, the second hook trailing the first by an inch and connected with Dacron line. The first hook is cut off at the bend. Marabou is then tied on both hooks. The fly is weighted at the head with lead barbells (1/16 ounce) or medium- to large-size bead chain. The flies are amazingly snag-free, often extremely effective, and take only seconds to tie.

Nymphs are usually the most effective way to fish the North Umpqua when the summer steelhead are sated and being particularly difficult. A very small weighted nymph, a number 8 or smaller, can be effectively cast upstream on a 12-foot leader and fished on a dead drift using a strike indicator.

The winter river temperature is typically forty-two to forty-eight degrees. Joe recalls once taking a steelhead when the water registered a frigid thirty-seven degrees, and he feels that these Oregon steelhead are nearly dormant at that temperature. His line of choice is a fast-sinking shooting head with a four-foot leader, and his fly list begins with a 2/0 Muddler, "an excellent winter steelhead fly. I swing it on a shooting head and not necessarily very deep. The fly may be down only a couple of feet." Of his second choice, a 4/0 Skunk, he says, "I began using this size fly when I saw the driftboat guys doing so well with hot shots. When you're swinging a large fly, it's not much different from a hot shot, except, of course, it doesn't have the wobble to it."

When fishing dingy water, Joe likes to go to a big Polar Shrimp, General Practitioner, or the simple Silver Orange, a silver-bodied fly with fluorescent orange hackle and white bucktail wing. He prefers to fish his elegant spey flies whenever the conditions permit.

Brad Jackson, an outdoor writer and lecturer from Redding, California, originated the Ugly Bug, now a standard working fly for the North Umpqua. He first fished nymphs for steelhead in the 1970s, while working at Time Flies, Larry Simpson's fly-fishing store in Arcata, California. The pattern was Simpson's Rag Doll Nymph. "A Hare's Ear nymph hybrid," says Brad. "An alternative to conventional patterns sometimes found to be damagingly gaudy. Simpson insisted that active summer- and fall-run strains fed at times. Consequently, he believed that the fish responded much better to trout tactics and impressionistic nymph patterns than to traditional steelhead patterns."

Brad tried dead-drifting a few of his own nymph designs, with exciting but inconsistent results. Two summers of guiding out of Jim Danskin's Tackle Shop in West Yellowstone led Brad to a Pteronarcys nymph of his own design, Brad's Stonefly Nymph. It was heavily weighted and had rubber feelers. When Brad opened his own business, The Fly Shop, in Redding, California, he regularly fished the upper Trinity for its steelhead. One afternoon, he dead-drifted his nymph exactly as he would have done on the Madison for Montana browns and hooked four steelhead in succession, including a seven-pound hen, a gigantic fish for the Trinity.

Brad remembers. "I was too inexperienced to recognize the implications of the dead-drift hook-up." Six years passed before he could settle in with the concept. He recalls one morning at Steamboat on the North Umpqua with Phil Haight, "the day it all happened."

When we reached the river after breakfast, I walked into the first pool, saw a fish flash deep in the green currents, and dropped my nymph about ten feet upstream of that spot. I threw slack, fed a little line and allowed the fly to penetrate the water column, and led the nymph past the steelhead. I'll never forget that moment, because what happened next validated years of theorizing and speculating. The fish flashed again, the tip of the floating line moved, and I set the hook crisply. One hundred twenty-five yards downstream and ten minutes later I landed that bright buck—with my nymph seated in the corner of its mouth.

I whooped it up. No swinging fly. No gaudy tinsel or Day Glo theatrics. No sinking line. Just a dead drifted nymph like I'd used for fat rainbows on the riffles of Hat Creek. Phil and I landed so many fish in the next two hours we were oblivious to the intensifying downpour.

They shared their discovery, giving flies to Kenny Gleason and Dennis Black. "We couldn't have done a better job of spreading the word if we'd hired a publicist. We had given our ugly bugs to two of the most experienced and talented steelheaders in the Northwest!"

Ugly Bug

Hook: Size 2-8; 2 is most popular size, with sizes 4-8 used to imitate instars. *Thread:* Black. *Body:* Small to medium black chenille. Taper to duplicate the natural Pteronarcys nymph. *Tail:* Two black rubber hackles, 8-10mm long. *Legs:* Three pairs, 6-20mm, each pair a single piece of black rubber hackle secured in the middle at right angles to the hook. Evenly space and figure-eight in place. Wind chenille forward over lead foundation. (Don't figure-eight chenille around legs.) *Antenna:* Tie off and secure two black rubber hackles at the head for antenna, 20-30mm long. Rubber tail, legs, or antenna can be longer if more action is desired.

Weight should be large-diameter lead. Double-wrap thorax to enhance aper. Use double wrap if fishing deep-holding water, single wrap for shallow riffles. (Brad says, "Matching amount of lead to water type is vital to fly's effectiveness.")

Variegated Ugly Bug

Same as original but chenille is variegated black/yellow, and tied in sizes 4-8. This is used to imitate the golden stonefly.

Annually since 1980, Dave Hall has averaged more than 120 days guiding and fishing on the North Umpqua. When not operating his Jade River Guide Service, he works as the Umpqua Feather Merchants Quality Control Supervisor, with world-wide responsibility to oversee the tying of flies.

Though this single river is much of his life, he says, "I don't call myself an expert; in fact, in over two decades of fishing here, I don't know any experts on this river's summer steelhead. There are no hard, fast rules that lend themselves to these fickle fish. I have seen many of the so-called legends, and for the most part, the majority of them are far better storytellers than summer steelhead fishermen. Most of them are not familiar with hundred-foot casts, roll casts of sixty to eighty feet, and tough wading. They don't take to being skunked, and on no other river have I seen egos as crushed as they get here on the North Umpqua."

Dave got into fishing these "buggy" patterns when standard, more traditional patterns were not working. "I'm not trying to match the hatch in any traditional sense," he says. "But these flies do represent insects prevalent in the North Umpqua, bugs that were part of the juvenile's diet at one time."

He continues, "The Hammerdown Caddis and Golden Stonefly are patterns I've been using for trout for years with great success. I just enlarged them to accommodate steelhead and varied some techniques in their presentation. The Flashback Nymph was a fairly standard all-purpose nymph pattern. As with the Hammerdowns, I enlarged it, and used some pearl Flashabou to give it sparkle. The Crawlers were an extension of the soft-hackle flies that I included in my buggy patterns. You'll notice all the flies use a soft hackle that when wet makes for lot of movement and a great silhouette. The silhouette is the key. It is far more important in clear water than color. I want a fly that moves and exaggerates its presence in the water, a fly that moves naturally and can be 'pumped' in the drift to add further action. This is a far better material than rubber legs, which I detest!"

Note: Heavily weighting nymphs is standard on the North Umpqua, because it is necessary to run a fly along the bottom of the holding channels. This is best accomplished with a floating line and a leader of fourteen feet or more. A strong back-mend gives the fly a few seconds to get down. The rod then leads the fly through the dead drift and swing.

Hammerdown October Caddis

Body: Sparkle blends 50% #39 crawdad orange, 50% #9 march brown. (Any rusty-colored dubbing OK.)
Tail: Dark grey or black deer hair.

Wing: Dark grey or black deer hair tied down one-third back.
Legs: Soft brown or furnace saddle hackle. Legs at least as long as the body.

Hall fishes the pattern weighted or unweighted in sizes 1/0 to 6, depending upon the type of water.

Golden Stone Hammerdown

Body: Sparkle blend #14 goldenstone or similar-colored dubbing. Rib with stripped stem of brown saddle hackle.

Tail: Natural deer hair.
Wing: Natural deer hair, tied one-third back.
Legs: Soft brown saddle hackle as long as body.

The pattern is tied weighted or unweighted, depending on the water. Hook size is 2-6.

Flashback Nymph

Body: Dubbed black rabbit; rib with pearl Flashabou.
Tail: Black saddle hackle and five to eight strands of pearl Flashabou.

Wing Case: Dark turkey tail feather.
Legs: Soft black saddle hackle, length of body; one strand pearl Flashabou each side, same length; tie in weighted sizes 2-8. ·

Natural Crawler

Body: Dubbed hare's mask to thorax. Rib with "smoke" larva lace to thorax.
Tail: Long black saddle hackle.

Legs: Black saddle, long and soft
Head: Danville #505. Use thread to tie in a small tag under the tail.

Black Crawler

Body: Dubbed black rabbit. Rib with larva lace to thorax.
Tail: Long black saddle hackle, 5-8 strands.
Thorax: Black rabbit.

Legs: Black saddle, long and soft.
Head: Danville #505. Thread ties small tag under tail. Tied in weighted sizes 2-8.

No other steelhead river entertains so many fly fishing methods and demands such a variety of fly dressings as does the North Umpqua. The result is a steelheading mystique many layers deep, a sport embraced along its riffles, glides, and ledge rock pools in wonderful and innovative ways.

Page 17: PEPPERED DUCK BREAST/MARIONBERRY CATSUP and WILD RICE PANCAKES
Left: SESAME GINGER WAFERS and COCONUT CORNMEAL WAFERS
Above: CHICKEN and BLACK BEAN CHILI

Previous pages: BRUNCH at the STEAMBOAT INN with the North Umpqua beyond

Above: FROZEN ORANGE MOUSSE with BLACKBERRIES

Above: SOUR CREAM ROLLUPS with STRAWBERRY-RHUBARB JAM

Following page: RASPBERRY-RHUBARB PIES

Brunches

◆ ◆ ◆

FILBERT BEIGNETS
with BROWN SUGAR-ORANGE SAUCE

CORNMEAL, BACON, and PECAN PANCAKES

SOUR CREAM ROLLUPS

SHRIMP and PARSLEY CAKES
with ROASTED SHALLOT SAUCE

POACHED EGGS on SMOKED SALMON POLENTA
with SUN-DRIED TOMATO BUTTER SAUCE

TURKEY and DRIED APPLE SAUSAGE

NO-GLUTEN CORNMEAL MUFFINS

INDIVIDUAL CRAB SOUFFLÉS
with PARSLEY SAUCE

SPAGHETTI SQUASH PANCAKES
with SAFFRON SAUCE

SPINACH MUSHROOM ROULADE
with CHICKEN FILLING and SABAYON SAUCE

APRICOT-PECAN SCONES

CRANBERRY-APPLE STRUDEL

WALNUT, APRICOT, and PRUNE BREAD
with ORANGE-HONEY BUTTER

SWEET POTATO and PECAN SOUFFLÉ

BLUEBERRY CORNMEAL CAKE

SCALLOP FLAN

CHICKEN, FLANK STEAK, and TORTILLA "GÂTEAU"

ORANGE-FILBERT SWEET ROLLS

LEMON-POPPY SEED MUFFINS

DRIED CRANBERRY FRITTERS

SALMON QUENELLES with TARRAGON SAUCE

SOUR CREAM WAFFLES with SAUTÉED APPLES

FILBERT BEIGNETS *with* BROWN SUGAR-ORANGE SAUCE

This is our absolute favorite beignet recipe! A perfect brunch first course.

◆◆◆

1 recipe Brown Sugar-Orange Sauce
   (recipe follows)

◆

BEIGNETS

¹/₄ cup flour
5 tablespoons fine-ground toasted filberts
2 tablespoons butter
¹/₂ cup water
2 large eggs
2" vegetable oil in large-diameter pan

▲▲▲▲

Mix the flour and nuts together. Set aside.

Melt the butter in the water over medium heat. When melted, add the flour mixture all at once and stir well. Continue to stir over medium heat until the dough dries out and forms a ball, pulling away from the sides of the pan. Remove from the heat and set aside to cool for a couple of minutes. Then add the eggs one at a time—beating well after each addition.

Heat the oil to 350° in a large, heavy skillet or stock pot. (Test the temperature with a food thermometer or drop a 1" bread cube into the oil—it should quickly rise to the surface and begin to brown.)

When the oil is hot, drop the batter a tablespoon at a time into the oil. Turn the beignets over as they begin to brown on the bottom and cook until they are uniformly browned. Drain on paper towels; serve with warm Brown Sugar-Orange Sauce. Serves 6.

◆

BROWN SUGAR-ORANGE SAUCE

3 tablespoons butter
3 tablespoons orange juice
¹/₂ cup firmly packed brown sugar
1 tablespoon flour
1 egg, lightly beaten
1 teaspoon filbert liqueur (or vanilla)

▲▲▲▲

Melt butter in a small sauce pan. Add orange juice, brown sugar, flour and egg, mixing well. Cook over medium low heat until thickened, stirring constantly. When thickened, remove from heat and add the filbert liqueur. Set aside.

May be made ahead and carefully reheated prior to serving. Stores well in the refrigerator. Makes ³/₄ to 1 cup sauce.

CORNMEAL, BACON, and PECAN PANCAKES

In looking for a brunch pancake that would add texture to a menu, we came up with this recipe. Real maple syrup is a must!

◆◆◆

2-3 strips bacon
1/2 cup whole wheat pastry flour
1/2 cup cornmeal
    (preferably stone ground)
1 teaspoon baking powder
1/4 teaspoon baking soda
1/4 teaspoon salt
1/4 cup brown sugar
1/4 cup coarsely chopped toasted pecans
1 egg
3/4 cup buttermilk
1/4 cup oil
maple syrup

▲▲▲▲

Cook the bacon until crisp and drain on paper towels. Crumble the bacon (you should have a heaping 1/4 cup).

Place the bacon in a bowl and add the flour, cornmeal, baking powder, baking soda, salt, brown sugar, and pecans.

Beat the egg with buttermilk and oil and stir into the flour mixture with a few swift strokes. Cook on a hot griddle until nicely browned on both sides. Serve with warm maple syrup. Makes 8-10, 3″ pancakes.

SOUR CREAM ROLLUPS

As anyone who visits the Steamboat Inn knows, these are our house breakfast special—we couldn't remove them from the menu even if we wanted to without having a battle on our hands!

1 cup white flour
1 cup whole wheat flour
1/2 teaspoon salt
1 1/2 teaspoons baking powder
1 1/2 teaspoons sugar
1 1/2 teaspoons baking soda
2 cups buttermilk
2 eggs
2 1/2 tablespoons oil
2 cups sour cream
1 cup preserves, homemade or purchased
powdered sugar

▲▲▲▲

Combine the dry ingredients. Combine the buttermilk, eggs, and oil together and add to the dry ingredients, beating just until all is incorporated.

To cook on a griddle: Ladle out a 12″ strip of batter, using 1/2 cup of batter. Cook until the batter starts to bubble and firm up. Flip over to cook the other side.

To cook in a skillet: Pour batter in a round pancake shape and cook as above.

When pancake is finished cooking remove from pan. Spoon 1/3 cup sour cream along the pancake and top that with 3 tablespoons of preserves. Roll up in jelly roll fashion and top with a dollop of sour cream and jam. Dust with powdered sugar.

SHRIMP and PARSLEY CAKES with ROASTED SHALLOT SAUCE

You will have guests begging for more when you make these delicate cakes. Roasted Shallot Sauce is also good as a finish for sautéed chicken breast.

◆◆◆

1 recipe Roasted Shallot Sauce
   (recipe follows)

◆

SHRIMP and PARSLEY CAKES

3 tablespoons butter
3 large shallots, minced
1 large clove garlic, minced
3 cups parsley leaves,
   stems removed and chopped
1 cup fresh basil leaves, chopped
1/2 cup heavy cream
1 cup bay shrimp
1/4 cup fine dry bread crumbs
salt to taste
black pepper to taste

▲▲▲▲

Melt 1 tablespoon of the butter over medium heat in a non-aluminum pan. Add shallots and garlic. Cook until softened but not browned, about 3 to 4 minutes. Add the chopped parsley and basil, mixing well. Add the cream and cook until all but a tablespoon of the liquid is absorbed. Add shrimp and bread crumbs, mixing well.

Taste and adjust seasonings, adding salt and pepper as necessary. Set aside to cool.

When cool, shape into 4, 3-4" patties.

To cook: Melt the remaining 2 tablespoons butter in a skillet over medium heat and add the shrimp patties, cooking until lightly browned on the bottom. Turn and continue to cook in the same manner. Arrange on serving plates, top with Roasted Shallot Sauce, and serve immediately.

Depending on what course it is being used for, it will serve 2-4.

◆

ROASTED SHALLOT SAUCE

1/2 cup orange juice
1/4 cup roasted shallots*
6 tablespoons white wine
3 tablespoons raspberry
   or white wine vinegar
8 tablespoons cold butter
1/4 cup basil leaves, shredded
1 tablespoon heavy cream

▲▲▲▲

Pour the orange juice into a nonreactive saucepan and reduce to 3 tablespoons over medium high heat. Add the shallots, wine, and vinegar and reduce the mixture to 2 tablespoons.

Reduce the heat to low and whisk in cold butter—one tablespoon at a time—until all is incorporated. Stir in shredded basil and heavy cream. Set aside and keep warm.

See the Glossary for the directions for roasting shallots. You may use regular shallots if necessary.

POACHED EGGS on SMOKED SALMON POLENTA with SUN-DRIED TOMATO BUTTER SAUCE

This recipe is a "distant cousin" to the more common eggs Benedict.

◆◆◆

6 large eggs

1 recipe Sun-Dried Tomato Butter Sauce
    (recipe follows)

1 recipe Smoked Salmon Polenta
    (recipe follows)

▲▲▲▲

Set the eggs aside and proceed with making with the Sun-Dried Tomato Butter Sauce and Smoked Salmon Polenta.

◆

SUN-DRIED TOMATO BUTTER SAUCE

3 shallots, minced
2 tablespoons sherry wine vinegar
1 cup fish stock or bottled clam juice
$^1/_4$ cup sun-dried tomatoes, snipped,
    (dry pack, not packed in oil)
$^1/_2$ cup cold butter
pinch of black pepper

▲▲▲▲

Cook the shallots and vinegar in a nonreactive saucepan over medium heat until liquid has evaporated, 1-2 minutes (watch carefully).

Add fish stock (or clam juice) and sun-dried tomatoes and reduce to $^1/_4$ cup. Whisk the butter into the sauce 1 tablespoon at a time. Season with pepper to taste.

Set aside in a warm place.

◆

SMOKED SALMON POLENTA

1 cup buttermilk
2 cups unsalted stock,
    or 1 cup salted & 1 cup water
$^1/_2$ cup cornmeal, regular grind
2 tablespoons flaked smoked salmon

▲▲▲▲

Heat buttermilk and stock until it comes to a boil. Stir in the cornmeal and cook, stirring constantly, until the cornmeal is softened and is a creamy texture. Stir in the smoked salmon. Set aside and keep warm.

To assemble: Poach the eggs. Warm 6 plates and divide the Smoked Salmon Polenta among the plates. Top each with a poached egg and Sun-Dried Tomato Butter Sauce. Serves 6.

TURKEY and DRIED APPLE SAUSAGE

We created this recipe when we were looking for a brunch meat that was full flavored but less caloric and fatty than most sausages.

◆◆◆

1 tablespoon butter
1 cup onion, finely minced
2 cloves garlic, minced
1/4 cup snipped dried apples
1/4 cup chicken stock
1 teaspoon dried sage
1/2 teaspoon ground dried rosemary leaves
3/4 pound trimmed turkey breast, ground
1/4 pound ground pork
1/4 cup butter, softened
1 teaspoon salt
1/2 teaspoon black pepper
vegetable oil for cooking

▲▲▲▲

Melt the 1 tablespoon butter. Add the onion and garlic and sauté briefly. Add the snipped dried apples and the chicken stock and cook 1 minute. Remove from the heat and add the sage and rosemary. Cover and set aside until the apples have absorbed the liquid.

Meanwhile, combine the ground meats with the softened butter, salt, and pepper. Add the onion/apple mixture and mix well. Shape into patties.*

Heat a teaspoon or two of oil in a large skillet over medium heat. Add as many patties as the skillet will hold and cook until nicely brown. Turn the patties and continue to cook the other side until done. Continue with any remaining patties. Be careful not to overcook, or the sausage will dry out. Serves 4-6.

This recipe makes 1 1/2 pounds of sausage. We usually shape the mixture into 12, 2-ounce patties.

NO-GLUTEN CORNMEAL MUFFINS

The perfect alternative for someone who has an allergy to wheat products.

◆◆◆

1/3 cup ground roasted and salted sunflower seeds*
1 cup corn flour
3/4 cup brown rice flour
1/4 cup cornmeal
1 teaspoon baking powder
1 teaspoon baking soda
1/2 teaspoon salt
1 tablespoon dry yeast
2 tablespoons warm water (105-115°)
pinch of sugar
6 tablespoons butter, melted
1/3 cup maple syrup
1 cup buttermilk
2 eggs, beaten

▲▲▲▲

Preheat oven to 375°.

Combine the ground sunflower seeds, corn flour, rice flour, cornmeal, baking powder, baking soda, and salt. Set aside. Proof the yeast in the water with the sugar. As yeast is proofing, combine melted butter, maple syrup, and buttermilk. Add beaten eggs, mixing well.

Combine the buttermilk mixture and the yeast. Add to the flour mixture, stirring just enough to blend (the batter is thinner than many muffins, but will bake up OK). Divide the batter among greased muffin tins. Bake 15-20 minutes. Makes 12 muffins.

For variety, you may want to try adding 1/2 to 3/4 cup of any of the following: currants, raisins, dried cranberries, snipped dried pear, or any other manner of dried fruit.

Grind the sunflower seeds to the consistency of flour—breaking up any caking that may occur. A small blender jar works well for this quantity.

INDIVIDUAL CRAB SOUFFLÉS
with PARSLEY SAUCE

This is a worry-free soufflé that will be well received by your guests.

◆◆◆

6 buttered 1-cup ramekins
1 recipe Parsley Sauce (recipe follows)

◆

CRAB SOUFFLÉS

$^{1}/_{2}$ cup bottled clam juice
$^{1}/_{4}$ cup couscous
6 ounces fresh crab, chopped
2 tablespoons chopped yellow onion
2 tablespoons chopped
    red or green pepper
1 tablespoon minced fresh parsley
$^{1}/_{4}$ cup good quality mayonnaise
1 teaspoon Dijon mustard
$^{1}/_{2}$ teaspoon lemon juice
$^{1}/_{8}$ teaspoon cayenne
1$^{1}/_{4}$ teaspoon Tabasco™
2 eggs, separated

▲▲▲▲

Preheat oven to 350°.

Bring the clam juice to a boil in a nonreactive saucepan. Stir in the couscous and return to a boil. Remove from the heat, cover and let set 5 minutes. Fluff with a fork and set aside to cool.

Combine crab, onion, red or green pepper, and parsley. In another bowl mix together the mayonnaise, Dijon mustard, lemon juice, cayenne, Tabasco™, and egg yolks. Stir the mayonnaise mixture into the crab along with the cooled couscous.

Beat the egg whites until they are stiff but not dry. Gently fold them into the crab mixture. Divide soufflé among the buttered ramekins and bake 30-35 minutes. Remove from the oven, top with Parsley Sauce and serve. Serves 6.

◆

PARSLEY SAUCE

1 shallot, finely minced
1 clove garlic, finely minced
1 tablespoon balsamic vinegar
$^{1}/_{4}$ cup butter, melted
2 tablespoons flour
1 cup unsalted beef stock
1 tablespoon lemon juice
2 tablespoons minced roasted red pepper
2 teaspoons anchovy paste
pinch of cayenne
salt to taste
black pepper to taste
$^{1}/_{2}$ cup minced fresh parsley

▲▲▲▲

Combine the shallot, garlic, and vinegar in a nonreactive saucepan and cook until liquid is absorbed. Stir in the melted butter and flour, and bring to a simmer.

Add the beef stock and stir until thickened. Add the lemon juice, roasted red pepper, anchovy paste, cayenne, and salt and pepper to taste.

When hot and ready to serve, add the minced parsley.

SPAGHETTI SQUASH PANCAKES with SAFFRON SAUCE

These squash pancakes can also be substituted for the starch course in a dinner menu. They are especially good with barbecued meats.

◆◆◆

1 recipe Saffron Sauce (recipe follows)

◆

PANCAKES

3 tablespoons butter
3/4 cup minced onion
1 Anaheim pepper, remove seeds
   and membrane, then mince
2 tablespoons flour
1 medium tomato, seeded and diced
1/2 teaspoon salt
1/4 teaspoon black pepper
1 teaspoon curry powder
1 egg, beaten
3 cups lightly cooked spaghetti squash*
3/4 cup fine dry bread crumbs

▲▲▲▲

Melt 1 tablespoon of the butter in a pan over medium heat. Add the onion and Anaheim pepper and sauté 2 minutes. Sprinkle with the flour and continue stirring and cooking 2 more minutes until all traces of the flour have been incorporated.

Remove from the heat and stir in the tomato, salt, pepper, curry powder, beaten egg, and spaghetti squash, mixing well. Stir in 1/2 cup of the bread crumbs.

Form into 8 patties. Dip the patties in the remaining 1/4 cup bread crumbs, lightly coating both sides.

Melt the remaining 2 tablespoons butter in a large skillet and sauté the patties on one side until light brown, flip, and continue to cook other side until light brown. Remove from the pan and place on serving dishes. Serve with Saffron Sauce. Serves 4 to 8.

◆

SAFFRON SAUCE

2 tablespoons butter
2 shallots, minced
1 cup white wine
1 cup unsalted chicken stock
1 teaspoon saffron threads
1 1/2 cups whipping cream
1 teaspoon sugar
salt to taste
black pepper to taste

▲▲▲▲

Melt the butter in a nonreactive saucepan. Add the shallots and sauté until they start to soften. Add the white wine and stock and reduce to 2/3 of a cup. Add the saffron and whipping cream and cook until thickened and reduced. Taste, then add the sugar, salt, and pepper to taste.

To cook spaghetti squash: Carefully cut the squash in half lengthwise. Butter the cut edges and lay cut-side-down on a baking sheet. Prick the skin with a fork. Pour 1/2" water in the pan and bake in a 350° oven 1 hour (the squash meat should still have some texture to it—be careful not to overcook or it will get mushy). Scoop out and dispose of the seeds. Use a large fork to separate the squash meat into strands of spaghetti.

SPINACH MUSHROOM ROULADE *with* CHICKEN FILLING *and* SABAYON SAUCE

This is one of our "old standbys," used in brunch and luncheon menus.

◆◆◆

1 jelly roll pan, 10½″ × 15½″ × 1″
3 tablespoons butter, melted
6 tablespoons fine dry bread crumbs

▲▲▲▲

Line a 10½″ × 15½″ × 1″ jelly roll pan with foil and brush with the 3 tablespoons melted butter. Sprinkle the dry bread crumbs evenly over the butter. Set aside.

◆

SPINACH ROLL

30 ounces frozen spinach,
   thawed and squeezed dry
1 tablespoon butter
½ pound whole mushrooms,
   coarsely chopped and wrung
   in a towel to remove excess moisture
2 tablespoons minced green onion
2 cloves garlic, minced
2 tablespoons flour
¼ teaspoon dry mustard
¼ teaspoon thyme
dash of salt
dash of cayenne
½ cup grated Parmesan cheese, divided
5 egg yolks
7 egg whites
1 recipe Chicken Filling (recipe follows)
1 recipe Sabayon Sauce (recipe follows)

▲▲▲▲

Preheat oven to 375°.

Place the thawed and squeezed spinach in a medium bowl. Melt 1 tablespoon butter in a sauté pan. Add the mushrooms, green onion,

and garlic and sauté 2-3 minutes. Toss in the flour and stir until all is incorporated. Remove from the heat and add to the spinach along with the dry mustard, thyme, salt, cayenne, and ¼ cup of the Parmesan cheese, mixing well. Cool for a couple of minutes, then stir in the egg yolks.

Beat the egg whites until firm but not dry. Gently fold the whites into the spinach mixture. Spread the spinach mixture evenly in the prepared pan and top with the remaining ¼ cup Parmesan cheese.

Bake 15 to 20 minutes, until the spinach is firm to the touch. Remove from the oven and begin to loosen the foil along the long edge. Spoon the hot chicken filling over the baked spinach. Start along the long edge you have loosened, and roll up. (Return to a warm oven for 10 minutes or so to heat up if necessary.)

Cut the roll into 10-12 slices and serve with Sabayon Sauce.

◆

CHICKEN FILLING

5 tablespoons butter, divided
1 tablespoon minced garlic
3 whole chicken breasts, skinned,
   boned and cut into ½″ cubes
¾ cup minced onion
½ cup chopped celery
½ cup minced red pepper
2 tablespoons dry sherry
pinch of cayenne
2 tablespoons flour
1 cup chicken stock

▲▲▲▲

Melt 1 tablespoon of the butter and add a third of the minced garlic, sautéing briefly.

Add the chicken and cook until the chicken is just a bit pink in the center. Remove from the pan and set aside.

Melt 2 tablespoons of the butter in a skillet; then add the remaining garlic, onion, celery, and red pepper. Cook 3 minutes.

Return the chicken to the skillet along with the sherry and cayenne. Cook until chicken is no longer pink but is still moist.

Set aside.

Melt the remaining 2 tablespoons butter in a small saucepan. When melted stir in the flour and cook for 1 minute. Stir in the stock and continue to cook until the mixture has thickened. Stir into the chicken mixture.

Season to taste.

◆

SABAYON SAUCE

1 cup white wine
4 egg yolks
1 teaspoon thyme
2 tablespoons minced fresh parsley
2 tablespoons minced green onion tops
    or garlic chives
dash of salt
pinch of cayenne

▲▲▲▲

Combine wine and egg yolks in the top of a double boiler over simmering water. Stir constantly until thick. When thickened, add the seasonings. Keep warm until served.

APRICOT-PECAN SCONES

No collection of brunch recipes would be complete without scones! These are quick to assemble, delicate in texture and full flavored.

◆◆◆

1 cup flour
1 cup whole wheat pastry flour
1 tablespoon baking powder
6 tablespoons sugar
6 tablespoons cold butter
$1/2$ cup apricots, snipped
$1/2$ cup pecans, chopped
2 eggs
$1/4$ cup half and half

▲▲▲▲

Preheat oven to 375°.

Combine the flours, baking powder, and sugar. Cut in the butter. Stir the apricots and pecans into the flour mixture.

Beat the eggs and half and half together. Stir into the flour mixture.* Gather into a ball and turn out onto a lightly floured counter. Knead gently a few times. Roll out to $1/2''$ to $3/4''$ thick and cut with a biscuit cutter. Place scones on a lightly buttered (or parchment covered) baking sheet and bake for 12-15 minutes in the preheated oven.

Serve warm from the oven with butter and honey. Makes 8-10 scones.

For an alternative shape, drop by the spoonful onto the lightly buttered baking sheet. Bake as directed.

CRANBERRY-APPLE STRUDEL

This recipe does not hold very well and is best served on the day it is baked. As tasty as it is, you shouldn't have to worry about leftovers!

◆◆◆

1 jelly roll pan, 10½″ × 15½″ × 1″
1 recipe Pastry (recipe follows)

◆

CRANBERRY-APPLE FILLING

2 tablespoons butter
3¾ cups whole cranberries
6 tablespoons orange liqueur
    or ¼ cup orange juice
3 tablespoons grated orange zest
1¾ cups sugar
3 tablespoons cornstarch
6 medium Granny Smith apples
    (or other tart apples)
¾ cup chopped walnuts
¾ cup fine dry bread crumbs

▲▲▲▲

Melt the butter in a nonreactive saucepan over medium heat. Add the cranberries. Cook the berries until they begin to pop. Add the orange liqueur and continue to cook 2 minutes. Add the zest, sugar, and cornstarch, mixing well. Cook, stirring occasionally, until the mixture thickens. When thick, set aside to cool.

As the cranberries are cooking, peel, core, and slice the apples. Place the sliced apples and walnuts in a bowl and add the cranberry mixture, mixing well. Stir in the bread crumbs.

◆

PASTRY

2½ cups sifted flour
1 teaspoon salt
1 cup cold butter
1 egg, separated
⅔ cup milk
2 teaspoons sugar
dash of cinnamon
dash of nutmeg

▲▲▲▲

Preheat oven to 375°.

Combine the flour and salt. Cut in the butter. Mix the egg yolk and milk and stir into the flour mixture. Form into a ball and knead a couple of strokes. Divide the dough in half. Roll out half the dough into a rectangle to cover the bottom and sides of the jelly roll pan. Spread the apple mixture over the pastry. Roll the remaining dough out and cover the apple mixture. Crimp the dough together. Cut 4-5 holes in the crust.

Beat the egg white and brush on the top of the strudel. Sprinkle with sugar, cinnamon, and nutmeg. Bake 45-50 minutes. Remove from the oven and cool slightly. Cut into squares and serve. Serves 8-10.

WALNUT, APRICOT, and PRUNE BREAD with ORANGE-HONEY BUTTER

This bread makes wonderful toast—slightly sweet and crunchy!

◆◆◆

1 cup warm water (105-115°)
2 tablespoons yeast
½ cup brown sugar
2 teaspoons salt
3 tablespoons butter, room temperature
1¼ cups scalded milk
1 cup dried apricots, snipped*
1 cup dried prunes, snipped*
1 cup walnuts, chopped
2 cups whole wheat flour
4½ cups white flour
1 recipe Orange-Honey Butter
  (recipe follows)

▲▲▲▲

Scald the milk and set aside.

Combine the yeast and the warm water and set aside to proof for 3-5 minutes, until the yeast is bubbling nicely. Add the brown sugar, salt, butter, scalded milk, dried fruit, nuts, and whole wheat flour, mixing well.

Add 4 cups of the white flour and turn out onto a floured counter. Knead the dough, adding additional ½ cup flour as necessary, until it forms a ball and is no longer sticky. Place in an oiled bowl, cover, and let rise in a warm place until it has doubled in bulk.

Punch down and divide into 3 small or two large loaves. Knead the loaves briefly to shape and place in oiled bread pans. Let rise in the pan in a warm place until double in bulk. Bake in a preheated 350° oven 30-50 minutes, depending on the size of the pan.

◆

ORANGE-HONEY BUTTER

¼ cup butter, room temperature
2 tablespoons honey
3 tablespoons powdered sugar
zest from ½ of an orange
1 teaspoon Yukon Jack®
  or other orange liqueur

▲▲▲▲

Combine ingredients. This will store well in the refrigerator. Let the Orange-Honey Butter warm up a bit before serving if it has been refrigerated. Makes 6 tablespoons butter.

These will be easier to snip if they are tossed with a small amount of flour first—which prevents them from sticking to the scissors as you snip them.

SWEET POTATO *and* PECAN SOUFFLÉ

This rich and hearty soufflé is perfect for a winter brunch menu.

◆◆◆

1 6-cup baking dish, buttered

3 cups cooked and mashed
   sweet potatoes or yams*
3 tablespoons butter
$^1/_2$ teaspoon salt
$^3/_4$ teaspoon finely minced lemon zest
$^1/_4$ cup real maple syrup
$^3/_4$ cup chopped toasted pecans
2 eggs, separated

▲▲▲▲

Preheat oven to 350°.
   While the sweet potatoes are warm, add the butter, salt, lemon zest, syrup, pecans, and egg yolks, mixing well. Set aside to cool to room temperature. Stir well before adding the beaten egg whites.
   Beat the egg whites until stiff but not dry. Fold whites into the sweet potato puree. Bake in the prepared dish 40 minutes. Serves 6-8.

*2, 2-2$^1/_2$"-diameter yams provide 3 cups puree.

BLUEBERRY CORNMEAL CAKE

The cornmeal adds a wonderful and unique texture to this flavorful cake.

◆◆◆

1 10" pie plate, buttered

1 cup flour
$^3/_4$ cup cornmeal
1$^1/_2$ teaspoons baking powder
$^1/_2$ teaspoon salt
1 tablespoon minced orange zest
$^2/_3$ cup sugar
1 tablespoon orange juice
$^1/_4$ cup vegetable oil
2 eggs
$^1/_2$ cup low-fat sour cream or yogurt
1$^1/_2$ cups blueberries (fresh or frozen)

▲▲▲▲

Preheat oven to 350°.
   Combine the flour, cornmeal, baking powder, salt, and orange zest, mixing well.
   Mix together the sugar, orange juice, oil, and eggs. Add the sour cream and then the flour mixture, mixing until just combined. Fold in the blueberries. Pour into the prepared pan and bake in a preheated oven 40-50 minutes. Remove from the oven and let rest 5 minutes before cutting. Cut into 6-8 wedges and serve warm.

If using frozen blueberries, do not thaw. This cake also works nicely with fresh raspberries. If raspberries are used, you may need to increase the sugar just a bit—depending on the tartness of the berries.

SCALLOP FLAN

Even a beginning cook can achieve great success with this delicious flan.

◆◆◆

1 8" spring form pan
   (butter bottom and sides)
1 recipe Crust (recipe follows)

◆

FLAN

4 ounces cream cheese,
   room temperature
8 ounces scallops*
1 large shallot, minced
1 clove garlic, minced
1 tablespoon minced fresh cilantro
1 egg
1 tablespoon pickled ginger
   (or minced red pepper)

▲▲▲▲

Preheat the oven to 350°.

Using a food processor, blend the cream cheese and scallops until smooth. Add the shallot, garlic, cilantro, and egg. Blend to a smooth paste, stopping occasionally to scrap down the side of the bowl.

Pour into prepared crust. Bake 15 minutes, remove from oven, and sprinkle with pickled ginger. Return to the oven and bake another 5-10 minutes. Cut into wedges and serve. Serves 4-6.

◆

CRUST

1 cup flour
¼ teaspoon salt
6 tablespoons cold butter
1 tablespoon sesame oil
2 tablespoons plus 1 teaspoon cold water

▲▲▲▲

Combine the flour and salt. Cut in the butter. Mix the sesame oil and water together. Add the oil-water mixture to the flour and stir with a fork to combine. Gather into a ball. Roll out on a lightly floured board into a 9" circle. Line the bottom and 1" up the sides of the prepared pan. Refrigerate 15-30 minutes. Line pan with foil. Bake 10 minutes. Remove from the oven, discarding the foil. Let cool while you are preparing the filling.

If scallops are frozen when weighed, add a couple ounces; weight will be lost when they are thawed.

CHICKEN, FLANK STEAK, and TORTILLA "GÂTEAU"

A colorful and festive brunch entrée, one that is hard for anyone to resist.

◆◆◆

½ pound chicken breast,
    skinned, boned, thinly sliced
½ pound trimmed flank steak,
    thinly sliced across the grain

▲▲▲▲

Seal the sliced chicken and flank steak in individual plastic bags. Set aside.

◆

MARINADE

2 cloves garlic, minced
2 fresh jalapeño peppers,
    seeded and chopped
⅓ cup chopped yellow onion
½ teaspoon oregano leaves,
    dried, not powdered
¼ teaspoon crushed red chilies
¼ cup lime juice
¼ cup water
1 tablespoon olive oil

2 tablespoons olive oil
2 tablespoons minced fresh cilantro

▲▲▲▲

Combine first 8 ingredients in a nonreactive bowl, mixing well.

Add half of the marinade to each plastic bag with the meats and seal well. Marinate the meats at least 2 hours or overnight.

Heat 1 tablespoon of the olive oil in a skillet. Sauté the marinated chicken until just cooked through. Sprinkle with 1 tablespoon of the cilantro. Set aside to cool. Repeat the process with the remaining olive oil, marinated flank steak, and cilantro.

◆

GÂTEAU

12 flour tortillas, 10″
1 cup guacamole
1 cup sour cream, divided
    (½ cup per gâteau)
1½ cups shredded lettuce
½ pound Monterey Jack cheese, grated
1½ cups cooked black beans
1 cup seeded and diced
    fresh tomatoes
½ cup chopped olives
¼ cup chopped parsley

▲▲▲▲

To assemble: Lay a tortilla on a baking sheet and top with ½ cup guacamole. Cover with another tortilla and gently press together. Spread with a thin layer of sour cream and half of the cooked flank steak strips. Top with another tortilla, gently pressing together.

Spread with a thin layer of sour cream and top with ¾ cup shredded lettuce, a quarter of the cheese and another tortilla. Continue with a thin layer of sour cream and half of the chicken and another tortilla. Then make a layer using sour cream and half of the cooked black beans, ending with the sixth tortilla on top.

Garnish with sour cream, a quarter of the cheese, half of the tomatoes, half of the olives, and half of the chopped parsley.

Repeat the process with the remaining ingredients. Makes 2 gâteaus, each cut into 6-8 wedges.

ORANGE-FILBERT SWEET ROLLS

A wonderful Sunday morning surprise for guests. The filling and dough can be prepared the evening before and refrigerated. The next morning, 3 hours prior to baking, you should remove it from the refrigerator to allow the dough time to warm up and rise.

◆◆◆

1 recipe Orange-Filbert Filling
(recipe follows)
1 recipe Orange Glaze
(recipe follows)

◆

ROLLS

½ cup milk
1 tablespoon yeast
½ cup warm water
2 tablespoons sugar
1 teaspoon salt
4 tablespoons softened butter, divided
1 egg, lightly beaten
2 teaspoons finely minced orange zest
1 cup whole wheat pastry flour
2½ cups white flour

▲▲▲▲

Heat the milk to bring it to room temperature. Set aside.

Dissolve the yeast in the warm water. Set aside to proof for 5-8 minutes.

Combine the milk, yeast, sugar, salt, 2 tablespoons of the softened butter, egg, and orange zest, mixing well. Stir in the whole wheat pastry flour and 2 cups of the white flour. Add the remaining flour as needed to form a soft dough. Turn out onto a lightly floured board and knead until the dough is smooth, 5-8 minutes. Place in an oiled bowl and let rise until doubled in bulk.

While the dough is rising, prepare the Orange-Filbert Filling.

When the dough has doubled in bulk, punch down and turn onto a lightly floured board. Roll out into a 12″ × 18″ rectangle.

Spread the remaining 2 tablespoons softened butter over the bread dough. Top with the Orange-Filbert Filling. Starting with a long edge, roll up in a jelly roll fashion. Using a sharp knife, cut the dough into 1″ slices. Place cut-side-down on a baking sheet. Let rise 30 minutes in a warm place.

Bake 20-25 minutes in a preheated 350° oven. Remove from the oven and cool slightly. Top with the Orange Glaze. Serve warm or at room temperature. Makes 15 rolls.

◆

ORANGE-FILBERT FILLING

½ cup currants (or raisins)
¼ cup fresh-squeezed orange juice
1 cup coarsely chopped filberts
2 teaspoons finely minced orange zest
½ teaspoon nutmeg
½ cup brown sugar
1 teaspoon flour

▲▲▲▲

Soak the currants in the orange juice 20 minutes. Stir in the remaining ingredients and set aside. (This recipe may be made ahead and refrigerated). Makes enough filling for 1 recipe of rolls.

◆

ORANGE GLAZE

1⅓ cups powdered sugar
⅓ cup fresh-squeezed orange juice
1 tablespoon finely minced orange zest
1 tablespoon softened butter

▲▲▲▲

Combine all of the ingredients, mixing well. Pour over warm rolls. Makes enough glaze for 1 recipe of rolls.

LEMON-POPPY SEED MUFFINS

A hearty breakfast muffin. Be sure you make enough; people always seem to want more!

◆◆◆

2 cups flour
1/2 teaspoon baking powder
1/4 teaspoon salt
1 cup packed brown sugar
1/4 cup softened butter
3 eggs
1 tablespoon finely minced lemon zest
6 tablespoons poppy seeds
1 cup sour cream, regular or low-fat
2 teaspoons baking soda

▲▲▲▲

Preheat oven to 375°.

Combine the flour, baking powder, and salt. Set aside.

Cream the brown sugar and butter. Beat in the eggs, lemon zest, and poppy seeds.

Combine the sour cream and baking soda. Add to the batter alternately with the flour mixture, stirring just until combined.

Pour into a greased muffin tin and bake 15-20 minutes. Makes 12 muffins.

DRIED CRANBERRY FRITTERS

The dried cranberries in this fritter add a chewy texture and a tart sweet flavor.

◆◆◆

3/4 cup dried cranberries
1/4 cup cranberry liqueur
3 tablespoons water

1/2 cup sifted flour
1/8 teaspoon salt
1 tablespoon sugar
1 egg, separated
1/3 cup milk
1 1/2 teaspoons butter, melted

oil for frying
powdered sugar

▲▲▲▲

Combine the dried cranberries, liqueur, and water. Soak several hours or overnight.

Sift together the flour, salt, and sugar.

Beat the egg yolk, milk, and butter together. Add the sifted ingredients and the cranberry mixture, stirring just until blended.

Heat 2" of oil in a heavy-bottomed pan to 375°.

Beat the egg white until it is stiff but not dry. Fold the beaten white into the batter.

Drop the batter by teaspoonfuls into the hot oil and cook 3-5 minutes, until uniformly brown on all sides. Drain on paper towels. Dust with powdered sugar and serve immediately. Serves 4-6.

SALMON QUENELLES *with* TARRAGON SAUCE

Most of the whipping cream has been removed from this recipe without sacrificing flavor. The result is just a little denser than a classic quennelle.

◆◆◆

1 recipe Tarragon Sauce (recipe follows)

◆

QUENELLES

²/₃ cup milk
2 tablespoons unsalted butter
¹/₃ cup white flour
1 egg yolk
¹/₄ cup goat cheese
¹/₂ pound trimmed and skinned salmon
¹/₂ teaspoon salt
¹/₄ teaspoon white pepper
¹/₄ cup whipping cream
3 egg whites

3 cups clam juice
3 cups water
    (you may use all water)

▲▲▲▲

Bring the milk and butter to a boil in a medium saucepan. Add the flour all at once, stirring with a wooden spoon until blended. (The mixture will be extremely thick.) Cook over medium heat, stirring constantly, until the mixture is very dry, 2-3 minutes. Remove from the heat and let cool slightly.

Transfer the slightly cooled mixture to the work bowl of a food processor. Add the egg yolk, goat cheese, salmon, salt, pepper, and whipping cream. Process until the mixture is smooth. Transfer to a nonreactive bowl.

Beat the egg whites until stiff but not dry. Fold the egg whites into the salmon mixture. Cover tightly; refrigerate 8 hours or overnight.

Just before serving, bring the clam juice and water to a simmer in a large, shallow saucepan.

Using 2 tablespoons, shape the quenelle mixture into ovals. Drop the ovals into the simmering water and clam juice, without crowding. Cook 3-4 minutes per side. Using a slotting spoon, transfer to paper towels to drain. Arrange on serving plates and top with Tarragon Sauce. Serves 6-8.

◆

TARRAGON SAUCE

¹/₄ cup sake
1 tablespoon minced shallots
¹/₄ cup clam juice
¹/₄ cup unsalted butter
2 teaspoons minced fresh tarragon

▲▲▲▲

Combine the sake and shallots in a nonreactive saucepan. Reduce over medium heat until 1-2 teaspoons liquid remains. Add the clam juice and reduce to 1 tablespoon. Stir in the butter one tablespoon at a time. Set aside and keep warm until ready to use. Just before serving, add the minced tarragon. Makes enough sauce for 1 recipe Salmon Quenelles.

SOUR CREAM WAFFLES *with* SAUTÉED APPLES

There isn't any need to wait for a brunch occasion to try these waffles—they may end up as a Sunday morning ritual!

◆◆◆

6 tablespoons melted butter
⅞ cup flour
1 tablespoon sugar
½ teaspoon baking powder
¼ teaspoon salt
⅛ teaspoon nutmeg
¼ cup ground toasted filberts
¼ teaspoon baking soda
1 cup sour cream (or low fat plain yogurt)
2 eggs, separated
4-6 tablespoons heavy cream

▲▲▲▲

Preheat waffle iron to medium setting. Melt butter and set aside to cool slightly. Combine the flour, sugar, baking powder, salt, nutmeg, and filberts and set aside. Mix the baking soda with the sour cream (or low fat yogurt). Beat the egg whites until soft peaks form.

Combine egg yolks, melted butter, and the sour cream mixture. Add to the flour mixture. Stir in the heavy cream to lighten the batter a bit. Gently fold in the beaten egg whites.

Pour some of the batter onto the waffle iron and cook following the manufacturer's instructions. Remove and hold in a warm oven while you cook the remainder of the batter.

Serve with maple syrup and/or sautéed fruit (recipe follows).

Makes 4, 7" round waffles.

◆

SAUTÉED APPLES

2 tablespoons butter
1 pound Granny Smith apples,
   peeled, cored, and quartered
¾ teaspoon freshly grated nutmeg
½ teaspoon cinnamon
3 tablespoons honey
2 tablespoons apple juice

▲▲▲▲

Melt the butter in a heavy skillet. Add the apples and cook over medium heat until they begin to soften. Add the nutmeg, cinnamon, and honey. Cook until most of the liquid is evaporated. Add the apple juice, tossing to combine. Keep warm until ready to serve.

Makes topping for 1 recipe of waffles.

Lunches

◆ ◆ ◆

VENISON CHILI

CARROT-THYME SOUP

HOT and SOUR FISH SOUP

VEGETARIAN BURGER

OREGON BAY SHRIMP ENGLISH MUFFINS

*TURKEY CROISSANT SANDWICHES
with CRANBERRY RELISH*

SMOKED TURKEY and SHRIMP JAMBALAYA

CUMIN CRÊPES with EGGPLANT FILLING

CHICKEN and BLACK BEAN CHILI

MUSHROOMS and MARINATED PORK in PHYLLO

*SESAME SEED CRACKER BREAD
and SMOKED TURKEY SANDWICHES*

BASIL-CHICKEN KABOBS

SPICY CHICKEN and BLACK BEAN POCKET SANDWICHES

LAMB MEATBALL STEW

MINTED LAMB PATTIES in POCKET BREAD

TURKEY MEATBALL SOUP

SQUID, CORN, and TOMATO SALAD

FLANK STEAK and BAVARIAN BLUE CHEESE SANDWICH

*SHRIMP, BROCCOLI, and CORN GÂTEAU
with RED PEPPER-BASIL SAUCE*

SPINACH SALAD with PEARS and PEPPER ALMONDS

TURKEY NECTARINE SALAD

DEB'S TOMATO FLORENTINE SOUP

CORN and SCALLOP CHOWDER

VENISON CHILI

We discovered years ago the classic flavors of chili and wild venison are a perfect marriage.

◆◆◆

2-4 tablespoons vegetable oil
3 pounds venison round steak,*
   cut in 1/2" cubes
4 cups beef stock or water
2 bay leaves

3 small dried hot chili peppers,
   seeded and minced
5 cloves garlic, minced
3 tablespoons paprika
1 tablespoon chili powder
1 tablespoon sugar
2 teaspoons salt
1 teaspoon ground cumin
1 teaspoon dried oregano leaves
1/2 teaspoon ground black pepper
1/2 teaspoon cayenne
3 tablespoons cornmeal
1 cup beer

▲▲▲▲

Heat 2 tablespoons of the oil in a stock pot and brown the venison, adding more oil as necessary. Add stock and bay leaves. Cover and simmer 1 to 1 1/2 hours, until the venison is tender.

Add the chili peppers, garlic, paprika, chili powder, sugar, salt, cumin, oregano, and the black and cayenne pepper. Continue to cook for an additional 30 minutes over low heat, stirring occasionally.

Stir the cornmeal into the cup of beer; then slowly stir this mixture into the chili. Raise the heat and cook, stirring constantly, until thickened. (The chili freezes well.) Serves 6-8.

*The chili is wonderful when made with wild elk but also works well with beef round steak or sirloin.

CARROT-THYME SOUP

A creamed soup without any cream. In our cooking classes, we usually include a vegetable soup using this format. The students are always amazed at how delicious and simple it is.

1 tablespoon butter
1 tablespoon olive oil
1 1/2 cups sliced yellow onion
2 teaspoons minced garlic
1 1/2 pounds carrots, peeled and sliced
   into 1/4" slices (4 cups)
3 1/2 cups low salt chicken stock
1 cup champagne
   (if unavailable, use more stock)
1 1/2 teaspoons dried thyme leaves
   or 1 tablespoon minced fresh leaves
3 sprigs parsley
4 teaspoons sugar (final amount
   depends on sweetness of carrots)
1/8 teaspoon salt
1/8 teaspoon white pepper

▲▲▲▲

Melt the butter with the oil in a saucepan. Sauté the onion and garlic in the butter mixture until the onions are limp. Add the sliced carrots and toss to coat. Add the stock, champagne, thyme, parsley, and sugar. Simmer until the carrots are crisp-tender. Puree in small batches and return to the saucepan.

Reheat and season with the salt, pepper, and—if necessary—additional sugar.

Serves 4 as a luncheon course.

HOT and SOUR FISH SOUP

Years ago we were served an excellent hot and sour fish soup that we enjoyed so much we decided to create one of our own.

◆◆◆

2 teaspoons minced fresh ginger
2 teaspoons minced fresh garlic
1 cup finely julienned carrots
    (cut 1" long)
1 tablespoon hot chili oil

5 cups fish stock,
    or a combination of fish and chicken
1 teaspoon crushed red chilies

1 cup cooked small shrimp
1 cup each raw scallops
1 cup cleaned clams
1 cup red snapper
    (or other firm white fish)
$1/3$ cup potato flour
1 cup green peas
    (if using frozen, thaw)
2 tablespoons chopped fresh cilantro
1 tablespoon red wine vinegar

▲▲▲▲

Sauté the ginger, garlic, and carrots in the hot chili oil for 5 minutes or until the carrots are crisp-tender. Set aside.

Combine the stock and crushed chilies in a saucepan and bring to a boil. Reduce the heat and simmer 5-10 minutes, until the stock picks up a good amount of "heat" from the hot chili oil.

Strain to remove the chilies from the stock and return the stock to a 3-4 quart saucepan. Bring to a rolling boil and add the carrot mixture and the seafood. Reduce the heat and simmer until the seafood mixture is no longer transparent, about 10-15 minutes.

Stir in the potato flour, green peas, cilantro, and wine vinegar. Heat and stir until slightly thickened. Taste and adjust the seasonings. Serves 4-6.

VEGETARIAN BURGER

We have had many requests for our veggie burger recipe—here it is in its original form. Please take note of the quantity it makes!

◆◆◆

1 cup lentils
3 cups *cooked* pinto beans
3 cups *cooked* black beans
2½ cups millet
10 cloves garlic, minced
1 cup grated carrot
1½ cups minced onions
1½ tablespoons ground cumin
1 tablespoon curry powder
6 ounces tomato paste
6 cups water
½ cup Worcestershire sauce
½ cup water
6 tablespoons butter
4 tablespoons Chimi Churri Sauce
    (see Glossary)
1 teaspoon black pepper
½-1 teaspoon salt
½ cup nutritional yeast
⅓ cup gluten flour

▲▲▲▲

Preheat oven to 350°.

Place the lentils in a 6-8 cup bowl, and add water to cover the lentils by 1″. Microwave on high for 15 minutes. Check and stir half way through the cooking time.

While the lentils are cooking, combine the cooked beans, millet, garlic, carrot, onion, cumin, curry powder, and tomato paste. Add a bit of the water if the mixture seems too thick. Process in the food processor in small batches; turn out into a large, oiled baking pan. Add any remaining water to the processed mixture, along with the cooked lentils. Bake 1½ hours, stirring occasionally.

Add the Worcestershire sauce, ½ cup water, butter, and Chimi Churri Sauce. Add the pepper and salt to taste, mixing well. Cook an additional 15 minutes.

Remove from the oven and stir in nutritional yeast and gluten flour. When cool enough to handle, shape into patties*. (These patties store well in the freezer.) Makes 25 patties.

Lightly oiled hands make shaping patties easier.

OREGON BAY SHRIMP ENGLISH MUFFINS

A quick and easy luncheon course, this is as delicious as it looks!

◆◆◆

4 English muffins, split and toasted
2 cups fresh bay shrimp
1 teaspoon minced fresh cilantro
4 teaspoons minced fresh parsley
dash of salt
dash of black pepper
1 ripe avocado, thinly sliced
dash of hot sauce
1 cup shredded Tillamook
    Cheddar cheese

▲▲▲▲

Preheat oven to 375°.

Toss the bay shrimp with cilantro, parsley, salt, and pepper.

Lay the split, toasted English muffins on a baking sheet.

Divide avocado slices among the muffin halves and sprinkle with a dash of hot sauce. Top each with ¼ cup of the shrimp mixture, then 2 tablespoons of the shredded cheese.

Place in the oven just long enough to melt the cheese. Remove to a serving platter and garnish with the remaining parsley.

Serves 4-6.

TURKEY CROISSANT SANDWICHES *with* CRANBERRY RELISH

These are especially nice when served with a spinach and apple salad with chutney dressing.

◆◆◆

6 croissants, 2¹/₂ ounces each
  (we use honey-whole wheat)

1 recipe Cranberry Relish (recipe follows)

2 cups chicken stock
6 thin slices good-quality Swiss cheese
12 ounces thinly sliced cooked
  turkey breast

▲▲▲▲

Slice the croissants lengthwise and place on a large baking sheet. Warm the Cranberry Relish if it has been refrigerated. Heat the chicken stock in a shallow skillet, add the turkey, and heat. Be careful to avoid drying the turkey out.

◆

CRANBERRY RELISH

³/₄ cup water
12 ounces whole cranberries,
  fresh or frozen
³/₄ cup sugar
1 teaspoon grated orange rind
¹/₄ cup orange juice

▲▲▲▲

Combine the ingredients in a nonreactive saucepan over medium heat. Simmer until the liquid is absorbed and the ingredients reach a relish consistency. Remove from the heat.

If using immediately, keep warm; otherwise, cool to room temperature and refrigerate in an air-tight container (this stores well for several weeks in the refrigerator).
Makes about 1¹/₄ cups relish.

To assemble: Spoon a generous tablespoon of the Cranberry Relish on the bottom half of each croissant. Top with two ounces of the warmed sliced turkey, a slice of Swiss cheese, and the top half of the croissant.
Place in preheated oven just long enough to melt the cheese. *Do not overheat or sandwich will dry out.*
Remove from oven, place on serving dishes, and top each sandwich with an additional tablespoon or two of the Cranberry Relish. Serves 6.

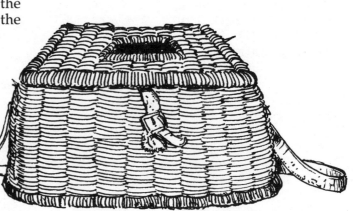

SMOKED TURKEY and SHRIMP JAMBALAYA

This needs only a crusty bread and a crisp salad to make all your guests very happy.

◆◆◆

1 1/2 tablespoons olive oil
1 cup raw brown rice
2 large shallots, minced
1/2 cup minced celery
2 cloves garlic
1 teaspoon salt (less if using
   canned chicken stock)
1/2 cup tomato sauce
7 cups chicken stock
1/4 teaspoon black pepper
1/2 teaspoon cayenne
1/4 cup minced fresh parsley
4 medium seeded red peppers, julienned
3/4 pound smoked turkey, 1/4" dice
1 pound medium shrimp,
   peeled and deveined
salt to taste

▲▲▲▲

Preheat oven to 350°.

Heat the oil in an oven-proof pan. Add the rice. Cook and stir until the rice is coated with oil. Add the shallots and celery. Cook until the shallots turn translucent.

Mash the garlic with the salt and add to the rice mixture. Add the tomato sauce, chicken stock, black pepper, and cayenne. Bring just to a simmer and remove from the heat.

Cover tightly and place in the preheated oven. Bake 30 minutes. Remove from oven.*

Stir in the parsley, red peppers, smoked turkey, and shrimp. Cover and return to the oven. Bake 10-15 minutes, until the shrimp are cooked through. Add salt taste. Serves 6.

The recipe may be prepared ahead to this point and refrigerated. When ready to serve, carefully reheat over medium heat. Then add the peppers, parsley, turkey, and shrimp. Cook until shrimp are pink and cooked through. Do not overcook.

CUMIN CRÊPES with EGGPLANT FILLING

The sour cream (or yogurt) garnish helps cool off these spicy crêpes!

◆◆◆

1 recipe Eggplant Filling (recipe follows)

◆

CRÊPES

2 eggs
$\frac{1}{2}$ cup corn flour
$\frac{1}{4}$ cup cornstarch
$\frac{1}{2}$ cup tomato juice
$\frac{1}{2}$ cup water
1 teaspoon ground cumin
pinch of cayenne
olive oil for cooking

Garnish:
    sour cream (or yogurt)
    avocado
    sliced green onion tops

▲▲▲▲

Place the eggs, corn flour, cornstarch, tomato juice, water, cumin, and cayenne in a blender jar. Process until combined.

Brush a 10″ skillet with olive oil; heat over medium high heat. Using a $\frac{1}{4}$-cup measure, spoon the batter into the skillet, tilting the pan to distribute the batter over the bottom of the pan. Cook one minute, turn over, and cook an additional 30 seconds.

Remove from the pan and place on waxed paper. Continue with the remaining batter, oiling the pan as needed. (These crêpes are best if they are used the day they are made.)

Spoon a portion of the Eggplant Filling onto each of the crêpes, garnish, and serve.

Makes 8, 8″ crêpes.

◆

EGGPLANT FILLING

$\frac{1}{4}$ cup olive oil
1 large yellow onion, chopped
2 garlic cloves, minced
1 large eggplant, about 1$\frac{1}{2}$ pounds
    (peeled and cut in small cubes)
1 red pepper, roasted and minced,
    or $\frac{1}{2}$ cup minced canned
        roasted red pepper
3 tomatoes, chopped
2 teaspoons ground cumin
1 teaspoon chili powder
1 teaspoon ground coriander
salt to taste
black pepper to taste

▲▲▲▲

Heat the olive oil in a nonreactive pan. Add the onion and garlic and sauté until softened and translucent. Add the eggplant and continue to cook until the eggplant is soft, about 15 minutes. Add the remaining ingredients, mixing well. Cook another 10 minutes to heat the tomatoes.

This filling can be made a day or two ahead. Serves 6-8.

CHICKEN and BLACK BEAN CHILI

This appears to be a long, involved recipe, but once the beans and chicken are cooked, it finishes off very quickly. (Both the beans and chicken can be prepared a day in advance.)

1 cup black beans
   (sometimes called turtle beans)
1 tablespoon ground cumin
2 bay leaves
6 cups water
1/2 teaspoon salt

2 1/2-pound whole chicken
1 small yellow onion, quartered
1 tablespoon crushed chilies

2 tablespoons olive oil
2 small yellow onions, finely chopped
3 cloves garlic, minced
1 cup bean cooking liquid
2 tablespoons minced Anaheim pepper
1 28-ounce can whole tomatoes,
   drain, reserving liquid, chop coarsely
3/4 teaspoon ground cumin
1 1/2 teaspoons chili powder
1/4 teaspoon crushed chilies
1 cup spicy stock

Garnish with any of the following:
   yogurt or sour cream
   minced cilantro
   parsley
   shredded cheese

▲▲▲▲

Cover the cup of black beans with water and soak overnight.

Drain the beans and rinse them a couple of times. Place beans in a small stock pot and add the cumin, bay leaves, water, and salt.

Cook over medium heat 1 to 1 1/2 hours, stirring occasionally, until beans are softened but not mushy. (You may need to add water to the beans as they cook.) When finished cooking, strain the beans, reserving the liquid.

While the beans are cooking, place the whole chicken in a stock pot. Add the onion and the 1 tablespoon crushed chilies. Cover with water, bring to a boil, and cook until the chicken no longer exudes pink juices when pierced with a fork, about 30-40 minutes. When finished, transfer to a pan and set aside.

Strain the stock to remove the onion and chilies. Return to the stock pot. When the chicken is cool enough to handle, remove the meat from the bones, returning the bones to the stock pot. Boil the stock and bones until the mixture is reduced by half. Strain and set aside.

Coarsely chop the cooked chicken.

Heat the olive oil in a small stock pot. Add the onions and garlic. Cook until the onions are soft but not brown. Add the cooked black beans and 1 cup of bean cooking liquid. Add the Anaheim peppers, the tomatoes and their liquid, cumin, chili powder, 1/4 teaspoon crushed chilies, the chopped chicken, and 1 cup of spicy stock. Heat and taste; adjust the seasonings. Pour into bowls and garnish. Makes 8 cups chili.

MUSHROOMS and MARINATED PORK in PHYLLO

The original version was a calzone, but the bread overpowered the filling. When we tried the lighter phyllo version, we all agreed it was a winner.

◆◆◆

16 sheets phyllo dough
olive oil spray or melted butter
fresh minced parsley
grated Parmesan cheese

1 recipe Marinated Pork
   (recipe follows)

1 recipe Mushroom-Pork Filling
   (recipe follows)

1 recipe Mushroom Sauce
   (recipe follows)

▲▲▲▲

Preheat oven to 375-400°.

Lay out one sheet of phyllo dough on a clean work surface.* Spray the sheet of dough with olive oil spray, sprinkle with a small amount of parsley and Parmesan cheese, and cover with another sheet of dough.

Working lengthwise with the dough, place one-eighth of the Mushroom-Pork Filling a quarter of the way down from the top edge.

Fold the top edge of the pastry over the filling. Fold the sides inward and roll up, spraying the final fold with olive oil spray to seal it. Place on an ungreased baking sheet and spray the tops. Continue with the rest of the filling.

Bake in a preheated oven 20 minutes, until golden brown. Transfer to serving plates, garnish with the Mushroom Sauce, and serve. Serves 8.

Note: Cover remaining phyllo dough with a piece of plastic wrap and a towel to prevent the dough from drying out. Any unused dough should be tightly wrapped and either refrigerated or frozen.

◆

MARINATED PORK

$3/4$ pound pork tenderloin, trimmed
$1/2$ cup Madeira
$1/4$ cup olive oil
1 clove garlic, minced
2 teaspoons Dijon mustard
$1/4$ teaspoon salt
dash of black pepper

▲▲▲▲

Thinly slice the pork as if for a stir fry. Place in a nonreactive bowl. Combine Madeira, olive oil, garlic, Dijon mustard, salt, and pepper. Pour over the pork. Mix well, cover, and let marinate at least 2 hours.

Drain the pork and discard the marinade. Sauté in a pan 3-4 minutes over high heat, stirring constantly, until the pork is no longer pink. Remove from the heat, drain off any pan juices, and set aside.

◆

MUSHROOM-PORK FILLING

2 tablespoons butter
2 tablespoons olive oil
2 cloves garlic, minced
2 shallots, minced
1 large leek, minced
    (use the white and 1" of the green)
1¼ pound mushrooms, sliced
2 tablespoons Madeira
1 roasted red pepper, chopped,
    or ½ cup chopped canned
        roasted red pepper
2 tablespoons minced fresh parsley
4 ounces Danish Fontina cheese, grated
salt to taste
black pepper to taste

▲▲▲▲

Melt the butter and oil in a large skillet. Add the garlic, shallots, and leek. Cook, stirring constantly, until the mixture softens. Add the mushrooms and Madeira, continuing to cook until the mushrooms are softened.

Stir in the red pepper, the Marinated Pork, and minced parsley. Mix well and add salt and pepper to taste. Set aside to cool. When cool, add the grated cheese. (May be prepared as long as a day ahead to this point.)

◆

MUSHROOM SAUCE

¼ pound whole mushrooms
2 tablespoons butter
1 clove garlic, minced
1 large shallot, minced
1 tablespoon minced roasted red pepper
2 tablespoons flour
1 cup chicken stock
1 teaspoon Worcestershire sauce

▲▲▲▲

Pop the stems out of the mushrooms. Mince the stems and combine with the garlic and shallots. Slice the mushroom caps.

Melt the butter and add the minced garlic, shallots, and minced mushroom stems. Sauté 2 minutes.

Add the sliced mushrooms caps and sauté until the mushrooms start to soften. Stir in the roasted red pepper, mixing well. Stir in the flour. Continue cooking and stirring until the flour is well incorporated. Add the chicken stock and the Worcestershire sauce, and cook until thickened. Taste and adjust seasoning.

SESAME SEED CRACKER BREAD and SMOKED TURKEY SANDWICHES

This bread, Armenian in origin, was introduced to us by our good friend, Kas McGregor, during one of her summer visits. It is available in delis or specialty food stores. The bread has a long shelf life, making it a handy pantry addition.

◆◆◆

1 large round cracker bread, softened*

1/2 cup dry-pack, sun-dried tomatoes, softened
4 ounces cream cheese
3 ounces goat cheese
1 clove garlic, minced
1-2 teaspoons hot sauce (we use Pico Pica®)
salt to taste
black pepper to taste

1/4 pound smoked turkey, thinly sliced
3/4 cup loosely packed basil leaves, coarsely chopped

▲▲▲▲

While the bread and tomatoes are softening, beat together the cheeses, garlic, and hot sauce. When creamy, add the salt and pepper to taste. Cover and set aside until ready to use.

When softened, drain the tomatoes, pressing with the back of a spoon to remove any excess moisture. Discard the liquid.

Remove the softened bread from the towel and place on a work surface. Spread the cheese mixture on the softened bread, working the mixture all the way out to the edges. Sprinkle the chopped basil leaves over the cheese. Scatter the softened tomatoes over the basil. Top with the thinly sliced smoked turkey.

Starting with the edge nearest you, tightly roll up the "sandwich."** Place the roll, seam side down, on your work surface. Using a sharp knife, cut off the ends on the roll to even them up. Slice the remaining roll into 1/2" slices. Makes 10-12 sandwich rolls. Serves 5-6.

To soften, dampen a large towel and lay on a counter. Run the cracker bread round under cold running water until both sides are thoroughly wet. (Do not let the bread get soggy—just wet!) Place the cracker bread on one end of the damp towel and fold the other edge over the wet bread to completely cover it. Set aside to soften for an hour.

**The sandwiches may be prepared ahead to this point. Wrap tightly in plastic wrap and refrigerate up to four hours. Then slice as directed above.*

BASIL-CHICKEN KABOBS

These are satisfying when served with teriyaki rice or a green salad as a luncheon course. They are also nice as a summer hors d'oeuvre.

◆◆◆

2 whole chicken breasts,
    skinned, boned, and cut in 1" cubes*
1/3 cup finely minced yellow onion
2 tablespoons minced fresh basil
1/4 cup low salt soy sauce
1/2 teaspoon sugar
1/4 teaspoon black pepper

1 red bell pepper,
    seeded and cut into 1" squares
1 yellow bell pepper,
    seeded and cut into 1" squares
1 medium yellow onion,
    cut into wedges
15 large fresh basil leaves

4-6 skewers

▲▲▲▲

Place the cubed chicken in a nonreactive bowl.
    Combine the onion, minced fresh basil, soy sauce, sugar, and black pepper. Pour over the chicken, cover, and refrigerate 2-4 hours.
    Prepare the barbecue grill.

Remove the chicken from the marinade. Wrap 15 chicken pieces with the large basil leaves. Arrange the wrapped chicken pieces, unwrapped chicken pieces, cut peppers, and onions on the skewers, alternating the pieces so the skewers are colorful.
    Barbecue over a hot grill for 5-10 minutes, turning the skewers occasionally. Serve warm. Serves 4 as a luncheon course.

Turkey breast will also work well in this recipe.

SPICY CHICKEN and BLACK BEAN POCKET SANDWICHES

If you like spicy foods, you will love this sandwich. The chicken breast and beans can stand alone as lunch, dinner, or picnic items.

◆◆◆

1 recipe Spicy Black Beans
   (recipe follows)

3 whole chicken breasts,
   skinned and boned

◆

MARINADE

¹/₂ cup olive oil
¹/₄ cup red wine vinegar
1 tablespoon minced Anaheim pepper
2 teaspoons minced jalapeño pepper*
3 tablespoons lime juice
1 tablespoon minced shallot
1 teaspoon salt
¹/₂ teaspoon black pepper

3 pita bread, cut in half and opened up
1 cup shredded lettuce or spinach
6 tablespoons sour cream,
   low-fat or regular

▲▲▲▲

Combine olive oil, vinegar, minced peppers, lime juice, shallot, salt, and black pepper in a nonreactive bowl. Add the chicken breast, cover, and marinate 4 hours.

While the chicken is marinating, prepare the Spicy Black Beans.

Prepare the barbecue. Grill the chicken breast 8-12 minutes, until no longer pink, but still moist inside.

Spread 1 tablespoon sour cream in each of the pita breads. Add ¹/₄ cup shredded lettuce or spinach, 1 chicken breast fillet, and some black beans to each pita pocket. Serves 6.

◆

SPICY BLACK BEANS

³/₄ cup dried black beans
boiling water
¹/₂ cup chopped yellow onion
2 cups chicken stock
1 dried pasilla chili
1 clove garlic, minced
1 small bay leaf
1 teaspoon ground cumin
¹/₂ teaspoon ground coriander
1 teaspoon dried oregano leaves
¹/₂ cup thinly sliced yellow or red pepper
1 tablespoon minced jalapeño pepper*
¹/₄ teaspoon cayenne
1 tablespoon hot sauce
   (we use Pico Pica®)
1 clove garlic, minced

▲▲▲▲

Place the black beans in a glass or stainless bowl. Add enough boiling water to cover the beans by three inches.** Set aside for two hours. After the beans have soaked, drain and transfer to a small stock pot. Add the onion, chicken stock, dried chili, garlic, bay leaf, cumin, coriander, and oregano. Bring to a simmer and cook, partially covered, until the beans are tender, about 1¹/₂ hours. Cool the beans in the cooking liquid. When cool, drain, and add the sliced peppers, minced jalapeño pepper, cayenne, hot sauce, and minced garlic. Makes 1¹/₂-2 cups cooked beans.

When working with hot peppers, be sure to wear plastic gloves and do not touch your eyes and face.

**Instead of soaking the beans in boiling water for 2 hours, you can soak them overnight in cold water.*

LAMB MEATBALL STEW

When the first hint of fall is in the air, it is time for us to make lamb meatball stew. It is one of those stews that warms the soul!

◆◆◆

2 pounds ground lamb
8 green onions, minced
½ cup minced fresh parsley
3 cloves garlic, minced
1 tablespoon ground cumin
⅓ cup grated Parmesan cheese
salt to taste
black pepper to taste
2 eggs

4 quarts lamb stock
1 cup barley

3 tablespoons olive oil
2 large yellow onions, minced
4 cloves garlic, minced
⅓ pound mushrooms, sliced
1 tablespoon Worcestershire sauce
1½ teaspoons curry powder
2 medium carrots, cut into small cubes
1 medium potato, grated
1 medium tart apple, grated

▲▲▲▲

Preheat oven to 375°.

Combine the ground lamb, green onions, parsley, garlic, cumin, and Parmesan cheese, mixing well.

Sauté 1 tablespoon of this mixture in a pan and taste for seasoning, adding salt and pepper as necessary.

Mix the eggs into the lamb mixture. Form into balls about 1" across. Place on a baking sheet (with sides) and bake in a preheated oven for 15-20 minutes. Remove from the oven and set aside.

Bring the stock to a simmer and add the barley. Cook 45 minutes. While the barley is cooking, sauté onions, garlic, and mushrooms in the olive oil until the mushrooms start to soften. Remove from the heat and set aside.

When the barley has cooked 45 minutes, add the onion mixture, Worcestershire sauce, curry powder, carrots, potato, and apple to the barley. Continue to cook until the carrots are tender. Add meatballs and cook until they are heated through. Taste and add salt and pepper and additional curry powder to taste. (This stew freezes well.) Serves 8.

MINTED LAMB PATTIES in POCKET BREAD

This is an interesting presentation for ground lamb, which we always seem to have in excess.

◆◆◆

1½ pounds lean ground lamb
3 cloves garlic
1 tablespoon minced fresh mint
1 tablespoon minced fresh sage
⅓ cup cornmeal
1 teaspoon salt
¼-½ teaspoon freshly ground
   black pepper
2 pocket (pita) breads,
   cut in half and opened

1 recipe Onion Marmalade
   (recipe follows)
      or
1 recipe Spinach Yogurt Sauce
   (recipe follows)

Garnish with the following:
   shredded spinach
   sprouts and/or
   tomato

▲▲▲▲

Combine the garlic, mint, sage, cornmeal, salt, and pepper in the bowl of a food processor or blender. Process until it all has the consistency of the cornmeal.

Combine ¼ cup of the cornmeal mixture and the ground lamb, mixing well. Shape into 4 patties. Dip each patty into the remaining cornmeal mixture, coating both sides.

Cook over medium heat 4-5 minutes per side until nicely browned on both sides and cooked through.

Serve in pocket bread with either the Onion Marmalade or Spinach Yogurt Sauce. Garnish with shredded spinach, sprouts, or tomato.

◆

ONION MARMALADE

1 tablespoon olive oil
2 cups coarsely chopped yellow onion
½ cup coarsely chopped medium leek
   (use the white and 1" of the green)
2 large shallots, coarsely chopped
2 tablespoons sugar
2½ tablespoons cider vinegar
salt to taste
black pepper to taste

▲▲▲▲

Heat olive oil in a heavy skillet over medium heat. Add the coarsely chopped onions, leeks, and shallots, mixing well. Reduce heat to low, cover the pan, and continue to cook until the mixture is soft, but not brown, about 30-40 minutes. Stir occasionally.

When onion mixture has softened, add the sugar and raise the heat to high to carmelize the sugar. When the onions/sugar mixture is brown, add the cider vinegar and cook until the liquid has evaporated.

◆

SPINACH YOGURT SAUCE

1 cup loosely packed fresh
   spinach leaves, chopped
2 green onions, cut in 1" lengths
⅓ cup nonfat yogurt
⅓ cup low-fat mayonnaise
2 teaspoons minced fresh mint
salt to taste
black pepper to taste

▲▲▲▲

Process the ingredients in a food processor, using the metal blade, until well blended. Add salt and pepper to taste. Refrigerate until ready to use.

TURKEY MEATBALL SOUP

There is no need to count calories when serving this hearty, satisfying soup.

◆◆◆

1 recipe Soup Base (recipe follows)

◆

MEATBALLS

1 pound ground turkey
¼ cup cornstarch
2 egg whites
3 tablespoons minced fresh cilantro
1 clove garlic, minced
1 teaspoon salt

▲▲▲▲

Preheat oven to 375°.

Combine all the ingredients except the Soup Base, mixing well.

Shape into ¾″ balls and place on an ungreased baking sheet. Bake in a preheated oven 15-20 minutes. Remove from the oven and set aside.

(May be prepared ahead and refrigerated for a day or frozen 2-3 weeks.)

◆

SOUP BASE

1 teaspoon olive oil
1 medium yellow onion, chopped
1 carrot, peeled and grated
1 stalk celery, chopped
1½ quarts turkey stock, divided
1 teaspoon minced fresh ginger
½ teaspoon ground cumin
½ teaspoon black pepper
3 tablespoons tomato paste
¼ cup corn flour
2 cups corn kernels, fresh or frozen
2 small tomatoes, chopped
⅓ cup chopped fresh cilantro
salt to taste

▲▲▲▲

Heat the olive oil in a stock pot and sauté the onion, carrots, and celery for 1 minute. Add 5½ cups of the stock, ginger, cumin, pepper, and tomato paste. Cover and simmer 25 minutes.

Mix the remaining ½ cup stock with the corn flour. Add to the stock pot and simmer until thickened. Add the corn and meatballs and heat through. Add salt to taste. Ladle into serving bowls and garnish with the chopped tomatoes and cilantro. Serves 4-6.

SQUID, CORN, and TOMATO SALAD

A colorful and flavorful salad that can be prepared year-round.

◆◆◆

1 recipe Salad Dressing (recipe follows)

2 small tomatoes, cut into wedges
4 cups shredded fresh spinach
¹/₂ cup seeded and diced tomatoes
2 tablespoons diagonally sliced
   green onion tops

◆

SQUID

1 pound small, whole squid (about 6)
1 tablespoon olive oil
2 teaspoons minced fresh garlic
1 cup corn kernels, fresh or frozen

▲▲▲▲

Mix the diced tomato and green onion tops in a nonreactive bowl. Set aside.

Clean the squid. Cut off the tentacles and set aside. Cut the narrower half of the body into ¹/₂″ rings. Split open the remaining half and score a diamond pattern into the squid with a sharp knife. Cut into 1¹/₂″ × 1¹/₂″ pieces.

Heat 1 tablespoon of the olive oil over high heat. Add the squid, stirring constantly for 2 minutes, until they begin to curl. Add the minced garlic and sauté another 2 minutes, stirring constantly.

Add the corn and cook 2 more minutes, until the squid is tender. Remove from the heat and strain in a colander.

Let cool to room temperature. Then add the cooled squid mixture to the tomatoes and green onion tops. Toss with the Salad Dressing to coat well. Divide the spinach among the salad plates, top with the squid, and garnish with the tomato wedges. Serves 4-6.

◆

SALAD DRESSING

2 tablespoons olive oil
¹/₂ teaspoon hot chili oil
2 tablespoons balsamic vinegar
2 tablespoons white wine vinegar
1 teaspoon sugar
¹/₂ teaspoon dried oregano leaves
1 teaspoon finely minced fresh garlic
¹/₂ teaspoon salt
¹/₄ teaspoon black pepper

▲▲▲▲

Combine dressing ingredients, mixing well.

FLANK STEAK *and* BAVARIAN BLUE CHEESE SANDWICH

One day, as we were extolling the delights of Bavarian blue cheese, we concluded it would match up well with flank steak in a sandwich. Here it is!

◆◆◆

1 2-pound flank steak, trimmed out

$^1/_4$ cup olive oil
1 medium yellow onion, sliced
2 cloves garlic, minced
5 tablespoons fresh lemon juice
2 tablespoons soy sauce
1 tablespoon Worcestershire sauce
2 tablespoons minced fresh ginger
1 tablespoon ground cumin
1 teaspoon chili powder
1 teaspoon dry basil leaves
1 teaspoon black pepper

6 tablespoons mayonnaise
8 slices sourdough bread
6 ounces Bavarian blue cheese

Place the flank steak in a ziplock bag and set aside.

Combine the next 11 ingredients and pour over the flank steak. Seal the bag, releasing any air. Place in the refrigerator overnight, turning occasionally.

Remove the flank steak from the marinade, reserving marinade, and set aside.

Prepare the barbecue. Then barbecue the flank steak until medium rare, about 7-8 minutes per side. (The cooking time will vary depending on the thickness of the steak.) Remove from the barbecue and thinly slice across the grain into long strips.

While the flank steak is cooking, pour the reserved marinade into a skillet and cook until all but $^1/_4$ cup of the marinade has evaporated. Reserving the juices, remove the onions from the pan and chop up.

Mix the mayonnaise and 6 tablespoons of the minced onions together.

Brush the underside of each slice of bread with the reserved pan juices. Place the slices, basted side down, in a couple of skillets. Divide the mayonnaise mixture among the bread slices and top with sliced flank steak. Divide the cheese among the sandwiches and heat until the bread is crisp on the bottom and the cheese melts. If necessary, you can put the sandwiches in the oven to finish melting the cheese. Serves 6-8.

SHRIMP, BROCCOLI, and CORN GÂTEAU with RED PEPPER-BASIL SAUCE

Don't let the long list of ingredients and instructions deter you from preparing this recipe. It is much easier than it may appear to be! Everything can be prepared in advance and popped into the oven for 20 minutes to finish this impressive dish.

◆◆◆

Shrimp Filling (recipe follows)
Broccoli Filling (recipe follows)
Corn Filling (recipe follows)
Red Pepper-Basil Sauce (recipe follows)

◆

CRÊPES

2 tablespoons butter
$1/2$ cup milk
$1/2$ cup water
$3/4$ cup flour
2 eggs
$1/4$ teaspoon salt
1 tablespoon minced fresh parsley
1 tablespoon minced fresh basil

▲▲▲▲

Melt the butter and set aside.

Combine the milk, water, flour, eggs, and salt in a blender and blend at high speed, stopping the blender to scrape down the sides of the jar to incorporate any stray bits. Continue to process a few seconds until all is well mixed. Pour out into a bowl and stir in the melted butter and minced herbs. Set aside to rest for 2 hours.

Brush a 10″ skillet with melted butter and heat over medium high heat. Using a $1/4$-cup measure, pour the batter into the skillet, tilting the pan to distribute the batter over the bottom of the pan. Cook one minute, turn over, and cook an additional 30 seconds.

Remove from the pan and place on waxed paper. Continue with the remaining batter, buttering the pan as needed.

They may be cooked a day or two ahead. Any leftovers freeze well and defrost quickly when needed.

Makes 8, 8″ crêpes.

◆

SHRIMP

2 teaspoons butter
1 small clove garlic, minced
$1/4$ pound medium shrimp,
    shelled and deveined
2 tablespoons minced fresh basil

▲▲▲▲

Melt the butter. Add the garlic and shrimp and cook until the shrimp turn pink and are no longer translucent when cut in half. Remove from the pan, add the basil, and set aside to cool.

◆

BROCCOLI

2 tablespoons butter
$1/4$ cup minced shallots
4 cups broccoli flowerets
    (peel and chop the stems)
$1/2$ cup chicken stock
1 cup grated Jarlsberg cheese
    (reserve $1/2$ cup to top the gâteaus)

▲▲▲▲

Melt the butter and add the shallots. Cook 1 minute until they begin to soften. Add the broccoli and stir to combine.

Add the stock and cover. Cook 2 minutes, just until the broccoli is crisp tender. Remove from the heat. When the broccoli has cooled a bit, chop coarsely and set aside.

When completely cool, stir in ½ cup of the grated cheese.

◆

CORN

1 tablespoon butter
¼ cup minced yellow onion
2 cups corn, fresh or frozen
2 tablespoons minced fresh parsley
salt to taste
black pepper to taste
½ cup clam juice*
1 tablespoon cornstarch

▲▲▲▲

Melt the butter and add the onions. Cook 1 minute until they begin to soften. Add the corn and cook 3 more minutes. Add parsley. Add salt and pepper to taste. Remove from the heat and set aside.

Combine the clam juice and cornstarch in a saucepan. Stir over medium heat until the juice thickens. Divide evenly among the shrimp, broccoli, and corn mixtures.

◆

RED PEPPER-BASIL SAUCE

2 tablespoons butter
2 cloves garlic, minced
½ cup minced roasted red pepper
   (about 2 large peppers)
¼ cup minced fresh basil
½ cup clam juice*
1 tablespoon cornstarch

▲▲▲▲

Melt the butter and add the garlic and sauté briefly until softened but not browned. Add the red pepper and fresh basil. Stir to combine. Set off the heat for a moment.

Combine the clam juice and cornstarch in a saucepan. Stir over medium heat until the juice has thickened. Combine with the red pepper sauce and heat briefly. Remove from the heat and set aside.

When ready to serve, return the red pepper sauce to the heat and cook an additional 2 minutes, stirring constantly. Set aside; reheat before serving.

To assemble (may be done 1 hour ahead): Place two crêpes side by side on a baking sheet. Divide the broccoli between the two crêpes, spreading the broccoli all the way out to the edge. Cover with another crêpe. Divide the shrimp and spread over the crêpes, topping each with another crêpe. Divide the corn in the same manner and top with another crêpe.

To bake: Preheat oven to 375°. Cover each stack of crêpes with foil and bake 10 minutes. Remove the foil and sprinkle ¼ cup of the reserved grated cheese over each stack of crêpes. Return to the oven and continue to bake for another 8-10 minutes.

Cut each gâteau into 4 pieces, place on a serving plate, and top with Red Pepper-Basil Sauce. Serves 8.

Clam juice often comes in 7⅞-ounce bottles— close enough to 8 ounces needed for 2 half-cups!

SPINACH SALAD *with* PEARS *and* PEPPER ALMONDS

The spiced nuts are a wonderful complement to the sweet and juicy pears.

◆◆◆

1 recipe Dressing (recipe following)

2 bunches fresh spinach,
   washed and stems removed
3 ripe pears
   (¹/₃ of a pear used in Dressing)
6 tablespoons coarsely chopped
   Pepper Almonds (recipe page 73)
¹/₄ cup thinly sliced red cabbage

▲▲▲▲

Cut 2 pears into 24 slices. Place in a small, nonreactive bowl; then toss with a small amount of Dressing.

Cut any remaining pear into small chunks, place in a separate nonreactive salad bowl and toss with a bit of the Dressing. Dry and tear the spinach, adding it to the pear chunks. Toss to combine.

Distribute the spinach-pear mixture among 8 salad plates. Top with red cabbage, the sliced pears, and spiced nuts.

Drizzle a small amount of Dressing over the salads and serve immediately.

Serves 8.

◆

DRESSING

¹/₄ cup rice vinegar
2 tablespoons sherry vinegar
¹/₄ cup vegetable oil
2 tablespoons walnut oil
1 tablespoon prepared mustard
   (coarse grain)
¹/₄ teaspoon salt
2 tablespoons honey
2 teaspoons sugar
¹/₃ of a pear, peeled

▲▲▲▲

Place all of the dressing ingredients in a blender jar. Blend well.

TURKEY NECTARINE SALAD

The combination of lean turkey breast and only one tablespoon of olive oil makes this a salad you can enjoy often without any pangs of guilt.

1 recipe Dressing (recipe follows)

4 cups cooked turkey*, sliced
2 ripe nectarines, pitted and sliced
1 bunch seedless grapes
1/2 cup toasted cashews
6 cups mixed greens, washed and torn

▲▲▲▲

Divide the mixed greens among 4 salad plates. Arrange the turkey, the sliced nectarines, and grapes attractively on top of the lettuce.
Sprinkle cashews over the top and drizzle 2 tablespoons of the dressing over each salad. Serves 4.

◆

DRESSING

1/4 cup fresh-squeezed lime juice
3 tablespoons balsamic vinegar
1 tablespoon olive oil
3 tablespoons honey
1-2 tablespoons minced
    crystallized ginger
1 clove garlic, minced
2 tablespoons minced shallots
3/4 teaspoons salt

▲▲▲▲

Combine Dressing ingredients and set aside.

We use a turkey breast prepared following the recipe for Spicy Turkey Breast (recipe page 99).

DEB'S TOMATO FLORENTINE SOUP

Deb Vanous, long-time employee and friend, prepares this soup for the "daytime" restaurant.

1 tablespoon olive oil
1 cup fresh mushrooms, sliced
1/2 cup minced onion
1/2 cup chopped celery
1/3 cup chopped green pepper
2 cloves garlic, minced
1 1/2 teaspoons dry basil leaves
1 teaspoon garlic powder
1/2 teaspoon salt
1/4 teaspoon black pepper
1/4 cup water
1 28-ounce can whole tomatoes
    drain, reserving juice, and chop
1 1/2 cups canned vegetable stock
1 cup V-8 Juice®
3 cups shredded fresh spinach

▲▲▲▲

Heat the olive oil in a medium-size stock pot. Add mushrooms, onion, celery, green pepper, and garlic. Sauté 5 minutes, until vegetables start to soften. Add the basil, garlic powder, salt, pepper, water, the chopped tomatoes and their juice, vegetable stock, and V-8 Juice.
Simmer 10-15 minutes to let the flavors meld. Taste and adjust the seasoning. Just before serving, add the shredded spinach and cook just until the spinach is wilted.
Makes about 9 cups soup, serving 4.

CORN and SCALLOP CHOWDER

This silky chowder also doubles very nicely as a tasty dinner entrée.

◆◆◆

2-4 slices crisp bacon,
    drained and crumbled—about ¼ cup
¼ cup minced fresh parsley

2 teaspoons butter
1 large potato, peeled and cut
    into ½″ dice (about 1⅓ cups)
1 cup minced leek
⅓ cup minced celery
3 cups corn kernels, fresh or frozen
1 cup half and half
2 cups milk
1 cup clam juice
8 ounces scallops, preferably bay scallops
    (if using large scallops, cut in quarters)
salt to taste
white pepper to taste

▲▲▲▲

Mix together the crumbled bacon and minced parsley. Set aside.

Melt the butter in a heavy, nonreactive stock pot. Add the potato, leek, and celery. Cook 5 minutes, stirring frequently. Puree 1 cup of the corn with the half and half. Add the pureed corn, whole corn, milk, and clam juice to the stock pot.

Bring to a low boil; then reduce the heat and simmer 30 minutes, until the potatoes are tender. Add the scallops and cook 3-5 minutes, until the scallops are cooked through. Season to taste with salt and white pepper.

Ladle into bowls, garnish with the bacon-parsley mixture and serve immediately.

Serves 4-6.

Picnics

◆◆◆

GRILLED CHICKEN BREASTS
with ROASTED GARLIC MAYONNAISE

ROASTED GARLIC *and* ROSEMARY BREAD

PEANUT DIP *with* FRESH VEGETABLES

PEPPERY COCKTAIL WAFERS

CURRIED LENTIL PÂTÉ

BROCCOLI NOODLE SALAD

GINGERED SWEET POTATO SOUP

SMOKED TROUT *and* PASTA SALAD

OMELETTE ROLL
with SESAME SPINACH FILLING

SPICY CUCUMBERS

"PIZZA" PICNIC BREAD

SMOKED CHICKEN *and* CURRY SALAD

MUSHROOM-FETA PICNIC BREAD

SHIITAKE MUSHROOM BREAD

GOAT CHEESE TORTA

SMOKED SALMON POTATO SALAD

MIDDLE EASTERN GARBANZO BEANS

PICNIC MUSHROOMS

ORZO *and* FETA SALAD

SPICY SHRIMP SALAD

LAMB STUFFED GRAPE LEAVES

SEEDED BREAD STICKS

DUCK *and* CHICKEN PÂTÉ

GRILLED CHICKEN BREASTS *with* ROASTED GARLIC MAYONNAISE

This is perfect picnic fare and also works well as an appetizer: slice the breasts and arrange over lettuce leaves on a serving platter. Pipe rosettes of roasted garlic mayonnaise over the sliced chicken. Garnish with fresh basil leaves. Serve with chardonnay.

◆◆◆

1/4 cup honey
1/4 cup vegetable oil
1/4 cup soy sauce
1/4 cup rum or brandy
6 large garlic cloves, chopped
6 whole green onions, chopped
1/4 teaspoon salt
3 lemons, cut into wedges
4 whole chicken breasts,
    skinned, boned, and cut in half
1 recipe Roasted Garlic Mayonnaise
    (recipe follows)

▲▲▲▲

Combine the first seven ingredients in a non-reactive bowl. Squeeze the lemon slices over the bowl; then drop into marinade. Add the chicken breasts, cover, and marinate at least 4 hours or overnight.

Grill over a medium flame 3 minutes per side, being careful not to overcook. Cool to room temperature. Serve with Roasted Garlic Mayonnaise. Serves 6-8.

◆

ROASTED GARLIC MAYONNAISE

1/2 cup good quality mayonnaise
3 tablespoons mashed roasted garlic
    (see Glossary)
2 tablespoons minced fresh basil
1 tablespoon minced sun-dried tomatoes

▲▲▲▲

Mix well. Refrigerate until ready to use.

ROASTED GARLIC and ROSEMARY BREAD

The title explains everything for this crusty picnic or dinner bread.

◆◆◆

1 tablespoon olive oil
2 teaspoons ground dried
   rosemary leaves
1½ cups warm water
1½ tablespoons dry yeast
1½ tablespoons sugar
1 teaspoon salt
5 cloves roasted garlic, mashed,
   about 1 tablespoon (see Glossary)
1 cup whole wheat flour
2½ cups white flour

▲▲▲▲

Combine the olive oil and the ground, dried rosemary leaves. Set aside.

Dissolve the yeast and sugar in the warm water. Add the olive oil and rosemary mixture, salt, roasted garlic, and whole wheat flour, mixing well. Set aside in a warm place to proof for 10 minutes.

Stir in the white flour. Knead 10-15 minutes until the dough is smooth and elastic, adding more flour to prevent the dough from sticking. Oil a bread bowl and add the ball of kneaded dough, turning to coat the dough with oil. Cover and let rise in a warm place until double in bulk, about 1 to 1½ hours. Punch down and divide into two pieces. Knead briefly and shape into 2 long loaves. Place on a cornmeal-dusted baking sheet. Let rise 30 minutes. Bake in a preheated 375° oven 25-35 minutes. Makes 2 loaves.

PEANUT DIP with FRESH VEGETABLES

A contrast of cool cucumber and this spicy dip is especially pleasing. Any picnic "leftovers" will be great to have on hand for impromptu gatherings.

◆◆◆

½ cup unsalted peanut butter
2 green onions, minced
6 cloves garlic, minced
⅓ cup low salt soy sauce
1 teaspoon minced fresh ginger
2-3 teaspoons hot chili oil
2 tablespoons honey
¼ cup sweet rice wine (Aji Mirin)
2 tablespoons minced fresh cilantro

Fresh vegetables:
   sliced cucumbers
   carrot sticks
   lightly steamed broccoli flowerets
   cauliflower

▲▲▲▲

Combine the dip ingredients, mixing well. When well covered and refrigerated, this dip will hold for quite some time.

Makes 1 to 1½ cups of Peanut Dip. Serve with fresh vegetables.

PEPPERY COCKTAIL WAFERS

These were developed to accompany a chardonnay at a wine tasting event. Due to their popularity and ease of preparation, we now keep them on hand to serve as an appetizer or to tuck in a picnic basket.

◆◆◆

¹/₂ cup butter
¹/₂ cup grated cheddar cheese
³/₄ cup flour
2 teaspoons paprika
¹/₂ teaspoon salt
¹/₂ teaspoon dry mustard
1 tablespoon sugar
1 cup ground Pepper Almonds
   (recipe follows)

▲▲▲▲

Cream the butter and cheese. Mix together the dry ingredients and the ground pepper almonds. Combine the butter and almond mixtures, mixing well. Divide the dough in half and shape each half into a 1" log. Wrap well and refrigerate. (The dough freezes well.)

When ready to bake, preheat the oven to 375°.

Slice the loaf into ¹/₄" slices and place on an ungreased baking sheet. Bake 10-15 minutes. Makes 60 wafers.

◆

PEPPER ALMONDS

2 cups whole almonds
1 teaspoon hot chili oil
¹/₂ cup sugar
¹/₄ teaspoon salt
1 teaspoon ground cumin
¹/₂ teaspoon cayenne

▲▲▲▲

Toast the almonds and keep warm until ready to glaze.

Combine the hot chili oil, sugar, salt, cumin, and cayenne in a medium-size heavy skillet.

Cook over medium high heat until the sugar melts and the ingredients are well combined. Add the warm almonds and stir until all of the almonds are glazed. Pour the almonds out onto a buttered baking sheet. Using the back of a large spoon, spread out to a single layer. Set aside to cool.

When cool, break into smaller chunks and store in an air tight container. Makes about 2 cups.

CURRIED LENTIL PÂTÉ

A vegetarian alternative that needs only a crisp cracker or crusty French bread to finish it off.

◆◆◆

1 can vegetable broth (14¹/₂ ounces,
   plus enough water to measure 2 cups)
¹/₂ cup lentils
1¹/₂ teaspoons ground cumin
2 large shallots, minced
1 clove garlic, minced
2 tablespoons nonfat yogurt
2 teaspoons balsamic vinegar
1 teaspoon curry powder
3 ounces smoked Gouda cheese

▲▲▲▲

Combine broth, water, lentils, cumin, shallots, and garlic in a small stock pot. Simmer for about 30 minutes, until the lentils are tender and most of the liquid is absorbed.

Transfer to a food processor and puree. Add the remaining ingredients and continue to process until all is well blended. Makes about 1 to 1¹/₄ cups pâté.

BROCCOLI NOODLE SALAD

When we serve this colorful salad, we are always prepared to fulfill recipe requests. There will be few leftovers from a picnic or potluck!

◆◆◆

6 ounces Japanese soba noodles
   or angel hair pasta
3 tablespoons sesame oil, divided
1 bunch broccoli, flowerets and stems
1 cup thinly sliced red cabbage
1 cup packed coarsely grated carrot
1/2 cup thinly sliced green onion
1/2 cup sliced almonds, toasted
1/4 cup vegetable oil
1/3 cup rice vinegar
3 tablespoons soy sauce
2 teaspoons minced fresh ginger
1 clove garlic, minced
few drops hot chili oil

▲▲▲▲

Cook noodles or pasta per package instructions. Drain, rinse, and toss with 1 tablespoon of the sesame oil. Set aside.

Cut broccoli into flowerets. Lightly blanch the flowerets in boiling salted water. Drain, then run under cool water to stop the cooking process. Drain again.

Peel and slice the broccoli stems. Combine the broccoli stems, blanched flowerets, red cabbage, carrot, green onions, and almonds in a nonreactive container.

Combine the vegetable oil, rice vinegar, the remaining sesame oil, soy sauce, fresh ginger, garlic, and chili oil. Mix well.

Add noodles and dressing to the vegetable mixture, mixing well. Taste and adjust the seasonings. Serves 6-8.

GINGERED SWEET POTATO SOUP

A thermos of this soup is the perfect complement for a winter ski outing.

◆◆◆

3 tablespoons butter
2 cups thinly sliced yellow onions
1 1/2 teaspoons minced fresh garlic
1 pound sweet potatoes or yams,
   peeled and cut into 1/2" slices
1 quart chicken stock
3 quarter-size rounds fresh ginger,
   minced
1/4 teaspoon salt
dash of black pepper

▲▲▲▲

Melt the butter in a 2-quart saucepan. Sauté the onion and garlic until limp. Add the sweet potatoes, ginger, and stock. Simmer until the potatoes are tender, about 20 minutes.

When tender, transfer the potatoes to a blender and puree until smooth.

Return to the saucepan and reheat. Add salt and pepper to taste, and serve. (This will freeze well. Do not be concerned if it separates; just stir and reheat gently.) Serves 4.

SMOKED TROUT and PASTA SALAD

The colorful pasta and smoked trout make this an interesting pasta salad variation.

◆◆◆

1 recipe Smoked Trout (recipe follows)

10 ounces spiral (Rotelle) pasta,
   mix of tomato, spinach, and plain
2 medium-size tomatoes,
   seeded and diced
$1/2$ cucumber,
   seeded and cut diagonally
1 cup coarsely grated carrot
$3/4$ cup minced fresh parsley
$1/4$ cup minced garlic chives
   or green onion
$1/2$ cup cubed red pepper
$1/4$ cup red wine vinegar
$1/3$ cup olive oil
1 tablespoon honey
2 teaspoons Dijon mustard
1 teaspoon salt
$1/4$ teaspoon black pepper
$1/4$ cup black lumpfish caviar

▲▲▲▲

Cook the pasta per the package instructions. Drain and cool.

Combine the cooled pasta, flaked trout, tomatoes, cucumber, carrot, parsley, garlic chives, and red pepper in a nonreactive bowl.

Whisk together the vinegar, olive oil, honey, Dijon mustard, salt, and pepper. Pour over the pasta, mixing well.

Taste and adjust the seasonings. Add the caviar just before serving. Serves 6-8.

◆

SMOKED TROUT

2 whole boned trout
   (about 8-10 ounces each)
$1/4$ cup olive oil
2 tablespoons lemon juice
1 teaspoon salt
$1/4$ teaspoon black pepper
$3/4$ cup cherry-flavor smoked chips
   (or other mild-flavored chips),
   soaked in water 30 minutes

▲▲▲▲

Cut the heads off the trout and discard. Cut the trout so they will lie flat. Place the trout in a nonreactive dish. Combine the olive oil, lemon juice, salt, and pepper. Pour the marinade over the trout. Let marinate 1 hour.

Prepare the barbecue. When ready, sprinkle the soaked chips over the coals. Place the trout skin side down on the grill.

Put the lid on the barbecue and close the vents. Let smoke for 15-20 minutes, until the fish flakes with a fork and is no longer opaque. Set aside to cool.

When cool, pick over the trout to remove any remaining bones. Yield should be about 4 to $4^1/2$ cups flaked trout.

OMELETTE ROLL *with* SESAME SPINACH FILLING

Our guests are always more than satisfied with this cold omelette.

◆◆◆

1 recipe Sesame Spinach Filling
   (recipe follows)

◆

OMELETTE

2 large eggs
2 tablespoons finely minced green onion
2 teaspoons finely minced fresh garlic
dash of salt and black pepper
1 teaspoon hot chili oil

▲▲▲▲

Whisk together the eggs, green onion, garlic, salt, and pepper. Using a 10" nonstick pan, heat the oil. Tip the pan to coat the entire bottom with hot oil. Pour in the egg mixture. Cook, lifting the sides of the omelet so the uncooked egg will flow under and cook.
   Makes 1 omelette.

◆

SESAME SPINACH FILLING

3 bunches fresh spinach,
   washed, stems removed
1/4 cup plus 1 teaspoon
   lightly toasted sesame seeds
3 tablespoons sweet rice wine (Aji Mirin)
1 tablespoon oyster sauce

▲▲▲▲

Cook the spinach in a nonstick pan just until it turns dark green. Remove from the pan and set on a towel to drain and cool. Chop the spinach. Blend sesame seeds, rice wine, and oyster sauce. Process to a paste. Stir into the spinach. Set aside. Makes filling for 3 omelettes.

To assemble: Turn omelette onto a plate. Cover with one-third of the Sesame Spinach Filling. Roll up like a jelly roll. Set aside to cool. Make additional omelettes. When cool, wrap tightly and refrigerate. To serve, unwrap and cut into 1/2" slices. Serves 4-6 as a picnic course.

SPICY CUCUMBERS

Reminiscent of a dish Pat was served in Japan, this dish was recreated with the help of our good friend Yoko Magness. Yoko cooks an occasional dinner at the Inn and also supplies us with her superb local lamb.

◆◆◆

1 cucumber, 8" long
coarse salt
3/4 teaspoon crushed red chilies
1 teaspoon minced fresh ginger
1/4 cup soy sauce
2 tablespoons sweet rice wine (Aji Mirin)

▲▲▲▲

Cut the cucumber into 1/2" slices and sprinkle with coarse salt. Set aside for an hour.
   Wipe the excess salt from the cucumbers and dry them. Put them between two layers of paper towel and lightly pound them with a rolling pin. Place the cucumber in a nonreactive container.
   Combine crushed red chilies, fresh ginger, soy sauce, and sweet rice wine. Pour over the cucumbers. Seal tightly and refrigerate. May be prepared one day in advance.

"PIZZA" PICNIC BREAD

We were trying to devise a name for this spiral bread when someone said, "Hey, this tastes like pizza" and, in fact, it does! So named.

⅓ cup warm water
1 tablespoon dry yeast
2 teaspoons sugar
1 teaspoon salt
1 cup buttermilk
1 teaspoon baking powder
1 cup grated sharp Cheddar cheese
1 cup whole wheat flour
2 cups white flour

1 recipe Onion-Caper Relish
   (recipe page 100)
3 ounces sliced pepperoni,
   cut in ¼" julienne
2 ounces Jarlsberg cheese, grated
1 beaten egg white

▲▲▲▲

Dissolve the yeast in the warm water with the sugar. Set aside 5-10 minutes until bubbly. Add the salt, buttermilk, baking powder, grated Cheddar cheese, and the flours.

Turn onto a floured board and knead until smooth and elastic. Add flour as needed to prevent the dough from sticking. Place in a greased bowl, turning the dough to coat it with oil. Cover and set in a warm place to rise until doubled in bulk, 1 to 1½ hours.

Punch the dough down. Knead briefly. Roll out on a floured board to a 12" × 17" shape.

Combine Onion Caper Relish, pepperoni, and grated Jarlsberg cheese. Spread over the dough.

Starting with the long edge, roll the dough up, pinching together. Pinch and tuck in the ends. Transfer to a baking sheet dusted with cornmeal. Let rise 30 minutes.

Brush with the beaten egg white. With a sharp knife or razor blade, lightly slash the top of the loaf.

Bake in a preheated 375° oven for 25-35 minutes. Remove from the oven and cool on a baking rack. Makes 1 large or 2 small loaves.

SMOKED CHICKEN and CURRY SALAD

Barbecue-smoked (see Glossary) or purchased smoked chicken will work for this salad.

◆◆◆

¼ cup pumpkin seeds
½ teaspoon curry powder

2 cups diced smoked chicken
1 cup diced celery
¼ cup thinly sliced green onion
½ cup minced red pepper

1 cup low-fat yogurt
½ teaspoon ground cumin
3½ teaspoons curry powder
2 tablespoons honey

12 slices cantaloupe
12 snow peas, lightly blanched,
   cut into diagonal slices

▲▲▲▲

Roast the pumpkin seeds and ½ teaspoon curry powder in a nonstick skillet until the seeds begin to pop and turn light brown. (Watch carefully as they have a tendency to burn easily.) Remove from the pan and set aside.

Combine the chicken, celery, onion, red pepper, and the roasted pumpkin seeds in a salad bowl.

Combine the yogurt, cumin, 3½ teaspoons curry powder, and honey, mixing well. Stir the dressing into the chicken mixture. Taste and adjust seasonings.

Garnish with the cantaloupe slices and the sliced snow peas. Serves 4-6.

MUSHROOM-FETA PICNIC BREAD

*You should let this bread cool, giving
the filling an opportunity to set up before you cut it.*

◆◆◆

1 recipe Mushroom-Feta Filling
  (recipe follows)

◆

BREAD

1 cup warm water
1 tablespoon dry yeast
1 tablespoon minced green onion
1 tablespoon minced fresh parsley
1 egg
¼ cup melted butter
1½ teaspoons salt
2 tablespoons brown sugar
¾ cup rye flour
3½ cups white flour
1 egg white, lightly beaten

▲▲▲▲

Dissolve the yeast in the warm water. Let set 5 minutes.

Add the minced onion, parsley, egg, melted butter, salt, and brown sugar, mixing well. Stir in the rye flour and 3 cups of the white flour. (Use the remaining ½ cup white flour for kneading.) Turn the dough onto a floured board and knead until smooth and elastic, about 10-15 minutes. Add flour as necessary to prevent the dough from sticking.

Place in a greased bowl, turning the dough to coat it with oil. Cover and set in a warm place to rise until doubled in bulk, about 1 to 1½ hours. While the bread is rising, prepare the filling.

After the dough has doubled in bulk, punch down and divide the dough into 2 pieces. Knead each piece of dough briefly and roll each out to a 12″×10″ rectangle. Spread half of the Mushroom-Feta Filling on each piece of dough. Roll up, pinching the dough together as you go.

Place the loaves, seam side down, on a cornmeal-dusted baking sheet. Let rise 30 minutes. Brush with the beaten egg white. Bake 25-35 minutes in a preheated 375° oven.

◆

MUSHROOM-FETA FILLING

1 tablespoon olive oil
1¼ cups minced yellow onions
1 tablespoon minced garlic
1 pound mushrooms, coarsely chopped
¾ cup loosely packed minced
  fresh parsley
½ cup chopped toasted walnuts
1½ cups crumbled feta cheese
1½ teaspoons dried thyme leaves
½ teaspoon salt
¼ teaspoon black pepper

▲▲▲▲

Heat the olive oil in a large skillet. Add the onions and garlic, cooking over medium heat 2-3 minutes. Add the mushrooms, stirring well. Cook, stirring frequently, 10-15 minutes, until the mushrooms have softened. Remove from the heat and stir in the remaining ingredients. Set aside to cool. (May be made ahead and refrigerated. Return to room temperature before using.)

Makes filling for 1 large or 2 small loaves.

SHIITAKE MUSHROOM BREAD

We developed this bread for our first book but did not include it feeling it was missing something. When we tried it with the onion marmalade, we realized we had found that "missing something."

1 recipe Onion Marmalade
    (recipe page 60)
softened butter (optional)

1 ounce dried shiitake mushrooms
1 tablespoon dry yeast
2 tablespoons molasses
1½ cups warm water
¼ cup powdered milk
1 teaspoon salt
2 cups whole wheat flour, divided
2 tablespoons sesame oil
⅓ cup minced onions
3 tablespoons oyster sauce
3-3½ cups white flour

▲▲▲▲

Soak the mushrooms for 30 minutes in enough boiling water to cover. When softened, remove from the soaking liquid, reserving the liquid. Squeeze mushrooms to remove any moisture. Snip off the stems and discard. Mince the mushrooms and set aside.

Dissolve the yeast and molasses in the warm water. Let proof 10 minutes. Add powdered milk, salt, and 1 cup whole wheat flour, mixing well. Let stand in a warm, draft-free place 30 minutes.

Meanwhile, heat the sesame oil. Sauté the onions and minced mushrooms for 2 minutes, stirring constantly. Add the oyster sauce and ½ cup of the reserved mushroom soaking liquid, mixing thoroughly. Cook an additional 2 minutes. Remove from heat and cool.

Combine the yeast and the cooled onion-mushroom mixture. Stir in the remaining 1 cup whole wheat flour and 2½ cups of the white flour. Add additional white flour until the dough is firm enough to knead. Turn onto a floured board and knead until smooth and elastic, 10-15 minutes.

Place in a greased bowl and turn to coat the dough with oil. Cover and set in a warm place to rise until doubled in bulk, 1 to 1½ hours.

When the dough has risen, punch it down and divide into two pieces. Knead each piece briefly to shape it and place in greased bread pans. Let rise until doubled in bulk.

Bake in a preheated 350° oven for 35-40 minutes. Remove from the pans and cool on a rack 10 minutes before cutting. (When making a sandwich, we spread the bread with straight Onion Marmalade. When serving the bread with a meal, mix 2 or 3 parts butter with 1 part Onion Marmalade, to taste.) Serve with Onion Marmalade. Makes 2 loaves.

GOAT CHEESE TORTA

While wonderful on a picnic, this is a perfect holiday appetizer with its red and green colors.

◆◆◆

1 6″ × 2″ round pan
    or mold of similar size
cheesecloth

1 teaspoon olive oil
1 tablespoon minced shallots
1 ounce sun-dried tomatoes, minced
2 tablespoons water
8 ounces cream cheese, regular or low fat,
    room temperature
8 ounces Montrachet goat cheese,
    room temperature*
2 tablespoons minced fresh parsley
¼ cup roasted salted sunflower seeds,
    coarsely chopped
½ cup fresh basil leaves, chopped

▲▲▲▲

Heat olive oil in a small, nonreactive skillet. Add the shallots and sun-dried tomatoes. Cook over medium heat, stirring constantly, for 5 minutes. Add the water and cook an additional 2-3 minutes, until the sun dried tomatoes are softened. Remove from the heat. Set aside to cool.

Using an electric mixer, cream the two cheeses until they are very smooth.

Cut enough cheesecloth for a double layer of cloth to line the entire pan and also to overhang the top of the pan. Wet the cheese-cloth and squeeze out any excess moisture. Line the pan with the cloth.

Divide shallot/sun-dried tomato mixture into two parts. Add the minced parsley and half of the chopped sunflower seeds to one portion. Line the mold with this mixture, pressing firmly into the bottom of the pan. Cover with half of the cheese mixture.**

Combine the remaining shallot/sun-dried tomato mixture with the chopped basil and the remaining chopped sunflower seeds. Spread over the cheese mixture in the pan. Top this with the remaining cheese mixture. Fold the overhanging cheesecloth over the pan and press firmly. Cover with plastic wrap and store in the refrigerator. May be made several days ahead.

If making ahead, take out of the pan after one day. Remove the cheesecloth, cover well, and refrigerate until ready to use.

To unmold: Remove the plastic wrap and fold back the cheesecloth. Invert onto a serving platter and carefully peel the cheesecloth off the torta. Discard the cheesecloth. The torta should be firm and will transport well in a picnic basket.

For a different flavor, or if you have difficulty finding the Montrachet, you may substitute feta cheese (Greek goat cheese) for the Montrachet.

***Place half the mixture between two pieces of plastic wrap and pat out into a 6″ round. Peel back the top piece of plastic wrap and invert the cheese round over the pan. Remove the plastic wrap and press the cheese mixture down and out to the edges, covering the tomato mixture.*

SMOKED SALMON POTATO SALAD

The variety of peppers makes this a stunningly colorful addition to a picnic.

◆◆◆

2$^1/_2$ pounds red potatoes, skin on
$^1/_2$ cup olive oil
$^1/_4$ cup vegetable oil
$^1/_4$ cup white wine vinegar
1 tablespoon minced fresh garlic
1 teaspoon salt
1$^1/_2$ teaspoons sugar
1$^1/_2$ teaspoons dry mustard
$^3/_4$ teaspoon black pepper
$^1/_2$ cup red pepper, $^1/_2''$ julienne
$^1/_2$ cup green pepper, $^1/_2''$ julienne
$^1/_2$ cup yellow pepper, $^1/_2''$ julienne
$^1/_3$ cup thinly sliced green onion
2 tablespoons minced fresh parsley
4 ounces smoked salmon,
   flaked, bones removed

▲▲▲▲

Cut the potatoes into $^1/_2''$ cubes. Add to a stock pot with water to cover, bring to a boil, and cook for 10 minutes. Turn off the heat, cover the pan, and let set 10-15 minutes, until the potatoes are tender.

As the potatoes are cooking, combine the olive and vegetable oils, wine vinegar, garlic, salt, sugar, mustard, and pepper, mixing well. Set aside.

Drain the potatoes and toss with half of the dressing. Let cool 10 minutes. Add the remaining ingredients and cool to room temperature. Add more dressing as needed. Serves 8.

MIDDLE EASTERN GARBANZO BEANS

An East Indian woman in graduate school with Sharon inspired the idea for this recipe.

◆◆◆

3 tablespoons butter
1 can garbanzo beans, 15$^1/_2$ ounces
1 clove garlic, finely minced
1 cinnamon stick
2 bay leaves
2 teaspoons curry powder
2 teaspoons cumin seed
salt to taste
$^1/_3$ cup sliced green onions
$^1/_2$ cup diced radishes
$^3/_4$ cup seeded and diced tomato
pita bread

▲▲▲▲

Melt the butter in a heavy skillet over medium heat. Add garbanzo beans and garlic. Sauté, stirring constantly, about 3-4 minutes. Add the cinnamon, bay leaves, curry powder, and cumin seed. Cook, stirring frequently, for 10 minutes. The beans should have absorbed the butter and will be starting to brown. Add salt to taste. Set aside to cool.

When the beans have cooled, add the green onions, radishes, and diced tomato, mixing well. Add salt as necessary. Serve with pita bread. Makes about 2 cups.

PICNIC MUSHROOMS

This dish will not add much color to a picnic but does bring with it a refreshing spiciness.

◆◆◆

1 tablespoon sugar
1 tablespoon rice vinegar
2 tablespoons low salt soy sauce
2 teaspoons hot chili oil
4 cups button mushrooms,
   stems cut flush with cap
1/2 cup seeded and thinly sliced
   Anaheim pepper
1 teaspoon finely minced fresh garlic
1 tablespoon pickled ginger
1 teaspoon sherry vinegar

▲▲▲▲

Combine the sugar, rice vinegar, and soy sauce. Set aside.

Using a nonstick fry pan, heat the hot chili oil. Add the mushrooms, Anaheim pepper, and garlic. Cook 1 minute. Add the sugar mixture and cook until the vegetables are well glazed and the liquid has begun to evaporate. Reserving the liquid, transfer the mushrooms to a nonreactive container. Reduce the reserved liquid by half.

Remove from the heat and add the pickled ginger and the sherry vinegar. Stir into the mushrooms. Cool to room temperature.

When cool, cover tightly and refrigerate until ready to use. Makes about 3 cups.

ORZO and FETA SALAD

This can be prepared in a matter of minutes and is always sure to please.

◆◆◆

1 cup orzo*
1/4 cup olive oil
1/4 cup lemon juice
2 tablespoons minced shallots
1 cup diced seeded zucchini
1/2 cup diced red pepper
1/2 cup crumbled feta cheese
1/4 cup toasted pine nuts
salt to taste
black pepper to taste

▲▲▲▲

Cook the orzo per the package instructions. While the orzo is cooking, combine the olive oil, lemon juice, and shallots. Drain the orzo and place in a nonreactive bowl. Add the zucchini and red pepper to the hot pasta, stir in the dressing, and cool to room temperature.

When cool, add the feta cheese and pine nuts. Season with salt and pepper to taste. Makes 6 cups, serving 4-6.

This rice-shaped pasta is also called Rosamarina.

SPICY SHRIMP SALAD

To maintain the freshness of the salad greens, make sure you pack the greens and shrimp separately and assemble them just prior to serving.

◆◆◆

1 recipe Dressing (recipe follows)

6 cups mixed salad greens,
    washed, torn, and spun dry**
1 ounce dry roasted or Spanish peanuts,
    chopped

◆

SHRIMP

12 ounces medium shrimp,
    peeled and deveined
1 clove garlic, minced
$1/8$ teaspoon black pepper
2 tablespoons diced yellow pepper
2 tablespoons diced red pepper
2 green thinly sliced onions
1 tablespoon grated Parmesan cheese

▲▲▲▲

Using a nonstick pan, cook the shrimp and minced garlic until the shrimp turn pink and no longer appear opaque when cut in half. Remove from the heat.

Combine cooked shrimp, black pepper, diced peppers, green onions, and Parmesan cheese. Pour some of the dressing over the mixture and toss well. Store in a nonreactive container until ready to use.

◆

DRESSING

1 clove garlic, minced
$1/4$ cup olive oil
4 teaspoons white wine vinegar
1 tablespoon lemon juice
2 tablespoons minced fresh cilantro
1 teaspoon minced jalapeño pepper*
$1/4$ teaspoon salt
black pepper to taste

▲▲▲▲

Combine garlic, olive oil, wine vinegar, lemon juice, cilantro, jalapeño pepper, salt, and black pepper. Mix well.

To serve: Lay the mixed greens on a plate and top with the shrimp mixture and chopped nuts. Drizzle any remaining dressing over the salads. Serves 4-6.

When working with hot peppers, be sure to wear plastic gloves; do not touch your eyes and face.

**Greens transport well in a sealed plastic bag.*

LAMB STUFFED GRAPE LEAVES

These are a great do-ahead picnic item. They can be held in the refrigerator for up to a week.

◆◆◆

1 jar grape leaves

1 pound lean ground lamb

2 teaspoons walnut oil
^{2}/$_3$ cup minced yellow onion
2 small cloves garlic, minced
^{1}/$_2$ cup chopped walnuts
^{1}/$_2$ cup tomato paste, divided
^{1}/$_2$ cup uncooked, short-grain rice
1^1/$_4$ teaspoons salt
^{1}/$_4$ teaspoon black pepper
1 cup plus 6 tablespoons lamb
   or beef stock, divided
walnut oil

▲▲▲▲

Drain and rinse the grape leaves and snip off any stems.

Using a nonstick skillet, sauté the onion and garlic in the walnut oil until lightly browned. Add the chopped walnuts and continue to cook 3 minutes, stirring constantly.

In a nonreactive bowl, combine the ground lamb, sautéed mixture, 6 tablespoons tomato paste, uncooked rice, salt, black pepper, and 6 tablespoons of the stock. Mix well.

Line a 9″ × 13″ casserole dish with several grape leaves.
Preheat oven to 350°.

To assemble: Lay several grape leaves on a work surface, vein side up.

Place 1 tablespoon filling ^{1}/$_2$″ up from the stem end. Fold the stem end of the leaf over the filling. Fold in the sides and roll up. Place seam side down in the baking dish. Continue with the remaining filling. (Tightly wrap any unused grape leaves and refrigerate.)

Combine the remaining stock, remaining tomato paste, and a sprinkling of salt and pepper. Pour over the rolled grape leaves. Lightly sprinkle with walnut oil. Cover tightly with two layers of tin foil. Bake in a preheated oven 45 minutes.

Makes 30-36 stuffed grape leaves.

SEEDED BREAD STICKS

These crunchy bread sticks are great alongside a dinner salad or packed in a picnic lunch.

²/₃ cup warm water
1 tablespoon yeast
1 tablespoon sugar
2 tablespoons vegetable oil
2 tablespoons olive oil
1 teaspoon salt
¹/₂ cup corn flour
¹/₂ cup whole wheat flour
1³/₄ cups white flour

2 eggs
1 tablespoon water
¹/₂ cup sesame seeds
¹/₂ cup poppy seeds

▲▲▲▲

Proof the yeast in the warm water with the sugar.

Add the oils, salt, corn flour, whole wheat flour, and 1 cup of the white flour. Add additional flour until you have a stiff dough. Turn out onto a floured board and knead until smooth and elastic. Place in a greased bowl, turning to coat all sides of the dough. Cover and let rise in a warm place until doubled in bulk. Punch the dough down.

Cut dough into 4 equal portions. Divide each of these into 8 pieces. Working rapidly, shape each piece into a long thin rop 10 inches long. (Start by rolling each piece in the palms of your hands, then finish by laying it on a flat surface and lightly rolling it with your fingertips until it is an even thickness.)

Mix the eggs and the 1 tablespoon water together and put it in a flat dish. Mix the seeds together and put them in another flat dish. Roll each rope of bread dough in the egg wash and then in the seeds. Place on parchment-lined baking sheets. Let rise in a warm place 30 minutes. (The dough can be made ahead and held in the refrigerator up to several days.)

Preheat oven to 325°.

Bake 20-30 minutes until golden brown. Makes 32 bread sticks.

DUCK and CHICKEN PÂTÉ

Serve with crackers or spread on crisp apple slices and dip the slices in toasted filberts.

◆◆◆

½ cup butter
1 medium yellow onion,
    thinly sliced
8 ounces chicken breast,
    skinned and boned
1 pound duck breast,
    skinned and boned
16 fresh basil leaves
5-6 tablespoons pan juices
6 tablespoons butter,
    room temperature
1 large clove roasted garlic
    (see Glossary)
12 small 1″ basil leaves
1 tablespoon pear brandy
⅛ teaspoon salt
2 pinches of white pepper

▲▲▲▲

Melt the butter in a heavy skillet. Add the onions and toss to coat. Cook until the onions are limp, about 5 minutes. Add the chicken and duck breasts and the fresh basil leaves. Cook 8-10 minutes over medium heat, turning once. Do not overcook.

Remove the breasts from the skillet and set aside. Strain the pan ingredients, pressing to release all the juices. *Reserve the pan juices.* Discard the solids.

Cut the breasts into chunks. Place in the work bowl of a food processor and process, using the metal blade, until the meats are ground. Add 3 tablespoons of the reserved juices, the softened butter, roasted garlic, basil leaves, pear brandy, salt, and pepper. Process until the mixture is smooth. If the pâté seems at all dry, add the remaining 3 tablespoons of pan juices. Taste and adjust the seasonings.

Makes 1½ to 2 cups pâté.

Dinners

◆ ◆ ◆

SMOKED SALMON STUFFED TROUT with TOMATO DILL SAUCE

ORIENTAL PORK with SESAME-CHIVE PANCAKES

LAMB MADEIRA STEW

EGGPLANT LASAGNE

BROCCOLI with SMOKED ALMONDS

*SPINACH and CHICKEN SAUSAGE
STUFFED FLANK STEAK*

PEPPERED DUCK BREAST with MARIONBERRY CATSUP

CHICKEN in PHYLLO

GRILLED LAMB CHOPS with PINOT NOIR SAUCE

TOMATO-GARLIC FRENCH BREAD

WILD RICE PANCAKES

CORN and JALAPEÑO CAKES with ROASTED RED PEPPER SAUCE

SPICY TURKEY BREAST with ORANGE and ROSEMARY

BARBECUED TROUT with ONION-CAPER RELISH

SCALLOPS in ONION-WINE SAUCE

BASIL GREEN BEANS

*MASHED POTATOES with ROASTED GARLIC,
BASIL, and SUN-DRIED TOMATOES*

BEET GREENS and MUSHROOMS

OVEN ROASTED or BARBECUED CHICKEN

BRINED and BARBECUED LEG of LAMB

PORCINI MUSHROOM RISOTTO

SESAME CORN

ONION and PEPPER BACON POTATOES

SPICY LAMB MEATLOAF

BULGUR with DRIED CRANBERRIES

BOBBY'S FRESH GINGER, LEMON, and HONEY YAMS

BUTTERNUT SQUASH with ONION and FRESH ROSEMARY

SPINACH and FRESH BEETS

GRILLED EGGPLANT and SQUASH with RED PEPPER MAYONNAISE

NAPA CABBAGE and CORN SALAD

POTATO GRATIN with FRESH SPINACH and MUSHROOMS

SMOKED SALMON STUFFED TROUT *with* TOMATO DILL SAUCE

If your trout is cleaned and deboned, this is an easy but impressive entrée. As with any fish, be very careful not to overcook the trout.

◆◆◆

1 recipe Tomato Dill Sauce
   (recipe follows)
6 whole cleaned and deboned trout,
   with heads removed (8-10 ounces each)

◆

STUFFING

6 tablespoons water
1/4 cup couscous
2 tablespoons olive oil
1/4 pound smoked salmon
2 medium shallots, minced
1 tablespoon mashed roasted garlic
   (see Glossary)
5 ounces cream cheese, softened
1/4 cup minced red pepper

1 egg white
2 tablespoons water
1/2 cup cornmeal
2 tablespoons olive oil

▲▲▲▲

Bring the water to a boil. Stir in the couscous and olive oil. Return to a boil, turn off the heat, cover, and let stand 5 minutes. Stir with a fork to fluff. Set aside to cool.

Flake smoked salmon with a fork. Combine flaked salmon, shallots, roasted garlic, cream cheese, red pepper, and cooled couscous.

Preheat oven to 375°.

Fill each trout with 1/6 of the stuffing mix. Beat the egg white with the water until frothy. Dip the trout in the egg wash, then in cornmeal. Heat 1 tablespoon of the olive oil in a large skillet. Lightly brown half the trout on both sides. Transfer the trout to a baking sheet. Continue with the remaining olive oil and the stuffed trout.

Bake 15 minutes in the preheated oven. Transfer to a serving platter and serve with the Tomato Dill Sauce. (Serve extra sauce at the table.) Depending on the size of the trout, serves 6-10.

◆

TOMATO DILL SAUCE

1/4 cup butter
2 tablespoons flour
1 cup clam juice or fish stock
1/4 teaspoon salt
dash of white pepper
1/2 teaspoon lemon juice
1 teaspoon dried dill weed
3 tablespoons tomato puree

▲▲▲▲

Melt the butter in a small, nonreactive saucepan over medium heat. Stir in the flour. Cook, stirring constantly, for 2 minutes.

Add the clam juice and bring to a boil, stirring constantly, until the sauce is thick and creamy.

Reduce the heat and stir in the salt, pepper, lemon juice, dill, and tomato puree. Cook an additional 3 minutes. Taste and adjust the seasoning. (This may be made ahead—cool and refrigerate until ready to use. Reheat just before serving.) Makes about 1 1/2 cups sauce.

ORIENTAL PORK *with* SESAME-CHIVE PANCAKES

This can be served as a main course for dinner or as part of a potluck or buffet. A pancake can be filled, folded like a burrito, and eaten standing up!

▲▲▲

1 recipe Marinated Pork (recipe follows)
1 recipe Mushroom-Pork Filling

◆

SESAME-CHIVE PANCAKES

2 eggs
$1/4$ cup nonfat dry milk
$1/2$ cup cornstarch
1 tablespoon sesame oil
$1/4$ teaspoon salt
$2/3$ cup water

2 tablespoons snipped chives
sesame oil for the pan
4-5 teaspoons sesame seeds
   (black sesame seeds add contrast)

▲▲▲▲

Combine the first six ingredients in a blender. Transfer to a small bowl; then stir in the snipped chives.

Rub a crêpe or omelette pan with a paper towel dipped in sesame oil.

Place the pan over medium high heat. When hot, add $1/4$ cup of the pancake batter. Immediately sprinkle the pancake with $1/2$ teaspoon sesame seeds. Cook about 1 minute. Flip over and cook 30 seconds. Transfer to a warm platter. Cook the remaining batter, lightly oiling the pan as necessary. (Pancakes will hold in a warm oven, or may be done ahead and reheated.) Makes 8 pancakes.

◆

MARINATED PORK

$1^1/4$ pounds trimmed pork tenderloin
$1/4$ cup sweet rice wine (Aji Mirin)
$1/4$ cup low salt soy
2 tablespoons rice vinegar
1 tablespoon oyster sauce
1 teaspoon sesame oil
2 large cloves garlic, minced
1 tablespoon minced fresh ginger root
several drops of hot chili oil

▲▲▲▲

Combine the sweet rice wine, soy sauce, rice vinegar, oyster sauce, sesame oil, garlic, fresh ginger, and hot chili oil. Pour over the pork. Place in a large ziplock bag and marinate overnight, turning occasionally.

◆

MUSHROOM-PORK FILLING

$1/2$ ounce dried shiitake mushrooms,
   softened*
$1/4$ pound stemmed fresh mushrooms
2 tablespoons sesame oil
3 whole green onions, minced
1 clove garlic, minced
1 medium red bell pepper, 1" julienne
2 cups bean sprouts
2 cups sliced napa cabbage
1 tablespoon low salt soy sauce
1 tablespoon oyster sauce
$1/2$-$3/4$ teaspoon hot chili oil
2 teaspoons cornstarch mixed with
   1 tablespoon sherry and
   1 tablespoon mushroom soaking liquid

▲▲▲▲

Drain the shiitake mushrooms, reserving the soaking liquid. Remove any hard bits of stem. Coarsely chop the mushrooms and set aside.

▲▲▲▲

Cut the fresh, whole mushroom caps into thick slices. Set aside.

Drain the pork, reserving the marinade. Slice the pork lengthwise into 3 or 4 strips; then slice the strips cross-grain into ¼" pieces. Set aside.

Place 2 tablespoons of the reserved pork marinade in a small skillet and sauté the chopped shiitake mushrooms for 2-3 minutes. Set aside.

In a wok or fairly large, heavy-bottomed skillet, heat 1 tablespoon of the sesame oil. Add the green onions and garlic. Sauté 1 minute, stirring constantly. Add the fresh, sliced mushroom caps, red peppers, and the remaining tablespoon of sesame oil. Cook, stirring constantly, over high heat until the mushrooms start to soften.

Add the shiitake mushrooms, bean sprouts, and napa cabbage. Cook an additional 3-4 minutes, stirring constantly. Transfer mixture to a warmed plate.

Place the pork and 2 tablespoons of the pork marinade in the wok and cook, stirring constantly, until the pork has lost most of its pink color. Add the reserved vegetable mixture to the pan and combine well. Add the soy sauce, oyster sauce, and hot oil. Stir and cook for 1 minute. Taste and adjust the seasonings.

Combine the cornstarch, sherry, and the mushroom soaking liquid. Add to the pork and cook until thickened. Transfer to a heated platter and serve with the pancakes.

*To soften the shiitake mushrooms, cover the mushrooms with hot water and set them aside for an hour.

LAMB MADEIRA STEW

This Lamb Madeira Stew, ladled over buttered Parmesan noodles and served with a green salad, is a quick and easy dinner.

◆◆◆

3 tablespoons olive oil
3 cups thinly sliced onions
1 tablespoon minced garlic
1 pound whole mushrooms,
　slice stems and quarter tops
2 pounds trimmed lamb stew meat
flour for dredging the lamb
1 cup stock or water
1 cup Madeira
2 teaspoons ground dried
　rosemary leaves
¾ teaspoon salt
¼ teaspoon black pepper
¼ cup minced parsley

▲▲▲▲

Heat 1 tablespoon of the olive oil in a heavy saucepan. Sauté the onions and garlic until softened. Add the mushrooms, and toss to combine. Stirring frequently, continue to cook until the mushrooms start to soften. Transfer to a plate and set aside.

Lightly dredge the lamb in the flour, shaking off any excess flour.

Add another tablespoon of olive oil to the heavy saucepan. Brown half of the lamb. Set aside. Add the remaining tablespoon of olive oil to the pan and brown the remaining lamb.

Return the set-aside lamb and the mushroom mixture to the pan. Add the stock, Madeira, and rosemary. Bring to a simmer, scraping the bottom to loosen any browned bits. Cook until the lamb is tender and the stew has thickened, 15-20 minutes.

Season with salt and pepper, and toss in the minced parsley. Ladle over buttered noodles and serve. Serves 4-6.

EGGPLANT LASAGNE

A vegetarian entrée that even the heartiest of meat eaters will enjoy.

◆◆◆

1 9″ × 9″ nonreactive baking pan

5 tablespoons olive oil
4 cloves garlic, minced
1 eggplant, 1¾-2 pounds,
    peeled, cut in ½″ slices
⅓ cup minced onion
3½ cups tomato sauce
1 tablespoon sugar
1 tablespoon dried oregano leaves
⅛ teaspoon salt
⅛ teaspoon black pepper
2 tablespoons tomato paste
2 tablespoons pesto
2 ounces Montrachet goat cheese
¼ cup grated Parmesan cheese
6 tablespoons grated mozzarella
    or Monterey Jack cheese

▲▲▲▲

Preheat oven to 400°.

Combine 4 tablespoons of the olive oil and half the minced garlic. Lay the eggplant slices on a baking sheet and brush with the olive oil-garlic mixture. Bake until the eggplant has softened, about 20 minutes. Remove from the oven and set aside.

While the eggplant is baking, heat the remaining tablespoon of olive oil in a small saucepan, and sauté the onion and remaining garlic 2-3 minutes. Add the tomato sauce, sugar, oregano, salt, and pepper. Cook 10 minutes; then stir in the tomato paste. Cook over very low heat, stirring occasionally, until ready to assemble the lasagne.

To assemble: Pour a layer of the tomato mixture into the baking pan, covering the bottom of the pan. Cover with a layer of baked eggplant. Dot the top of the eggplant with a tablespoon of the pesto and sprinkle on half of the goat cheese. Sprinkle with half of the grated Parmesan and mozzarella cheeses.

Top with another layer of eggplant, then the pesto and goat cheese. Sprinkle the remaining mozzarella cheese on top; then cover with a layer of the tomato mixture. Sprinkle the top with the remaining Parmesan. Bake 20-30 minutes, until bubbling and heated through.

BROCCOLI *with* SMOKED ALMONDS

This combination will add a great texture to a menu. With these simple ingredients readily available, it can be prepared year-round.

◆◆◆

1 bunch broccoli
2 tablespoons butter
¼ cup finely minced onions
¼ cup whole smoked almonds,
    coarsely chopped
salt to taste
black pepper to taste

▲▲▲▲

Cut the flowerets off the broccoli and set aside. Peel and slice the stems.

Bring a pot of lightly salted water to a boil. Add the flowerets, and cook 10 minutes.

While the flowerets are cooking, melt the butter in a small skillet. Add the minced onions and the sliced stems. Cook, stirring occasionally, to soften the onions and stems.

Drain the broccoli. Toss the sautéed stems, flowerets, and chopped almonds together. Salt and pepper to taste.

Serve immediately. Serves 4-6.

SPINACH and CHICKEN SAUSAGE STUFFED FLANK STEAK

The visual effect of this dish, when sliced, is as pleasing to the eye as it is to the palate.

◆◆◆

1½-2 pound flank steak
½ cup red wine
2 tablespoons soy sauce
1 tablespoon brandy
1 tablespoon Madeira
½ medium onion
4 cloves garlic
½ teaspoon salt

2 chicken apple sausages*

2 tablespoons olive oil
1 cup minced onion
4 cloves garlic, minced
¼ teaspoon black pepper
6 ounces Harvarti cheese, grated
¼ cup fine dry bread crumbs
20 ounces frozen spinach,
 thawed and squeezed dry

▲▲▲▲

Trim the flank steak. Then lay it on a cutting board with the grain running vertically as you face it. Using a sharp knife, start slicing the steak along one side. As you slice, peel the top back. Continue cutting until you are within ½" of the other side. When laid open, the steak will resemble an open book.

Set aside in a noncorrosive pan or seal in a plastic bag.

Combine the next 7 ingredients in a blender. Blend until onions and garlic are pureed. Pour over the flank steak. Cover and refrigerate the flank steak overnight.

Preheat oven to 375°.

Poach the sausages for 10 minutes in boiling water. Remove and set aside until the sausages are cool enough to handle. Peel off the casing and set the sausages aside.

Heat 1 tablespoon of the olive oil in a skillet. Add the onion and garlic, sautéeing over high heat until they are limp but not brown. Remove from the heat and add the pepper, cheese, bread crumbs, and spinach, breaking up any clumped-together spinach. Mix well.

Remove the steak from the marinade and discard the marinade. Dry the steak. Lay it out flat, cut side up, on a work surface.

Spread the spinach over the flank steak. Lay the sausages, end to end, along one edge of the steak, making sure they are running parallel with the grain of the steak. Starting along the edge the sausages are on, roll up the flank steak. (The grain should be running lengthwise.) Using heavy thread, tie the steak roll at intervals.

Heat the remaining tablespoon of oil in a heavy skillet. Brown the steak roll on all sides. Transfer to a rack set in a baking pan. Bake 30-40 minutes. Transfer the steak roll to a carving board and remove the string. Slice across the grain into ½" slices. Serves 4-6.

Found in most meat markets and delicatessens.

PEPPERED DUCK BREAST *with* MARIONBERRY CATSUP

With the Pepper Mix for the duck and the Marionberry Catsup prepared in advance, this can be finished in less than 15 minutes! This is nice with Wild Rice Pancakes (recipe page 97) and a green salad. Marionberry Catsup goes well with the pancakes also.

◆◆◆

2 tablespoons flour
1½ teaspoons Pepper Mix
    (recipe follows)
12 tablespoons Marionberry Catsup
    (recipe follows)
1½ teaspoons butter
1 tablespoon olive oil
3 whole duck breasts,
    skinned, boned, and cut in half

▲▲▲▲

Combine the flour and Pepper Mix. Lightly coat both sides of each duck breast half.

Gently heat the Marionberry Catsup and keep warm.

Heat the butter and olive oil in a skillet, and sauté the breasts for 3 minutes per side. They should be light pink and moist inside. Do not overcook. Transfer to dinner plates and nap each with 2 tablespoons Marionberry Catsup. Serve immediately. Serves 4-6.

◆

MARIONBERRY CATSUP

4 cups marionberries*
¼ cup butter
½ cup minced shallots
8-10 tablespoons brown sugar
    (amount depends on berry sweetness)
2 tablespoons balsamic vinegar
pinch of ground cloves

▲▲▲▲

Puree and strain the berries. You should end up with 2½ to 2¾ cups of puree.**

Melt the butter in a nonreactive sauté pan. Add the shallots. Sauté, stirring constantly, until softened.

Add the berry puree and 6 tablespoons of the brown sugar, mixing well. Cook over low heat 8-10 minutes, stirring occasionally. Add the vinegar and ground cloves. Taste and add the remainder of the brown sugar to taste. Let cook an additional 5 minutes. The catsup will have thickened slightly.

Remove from the heat and keep warm if using immediately. Otherwise, set aside to cool. When cool, refrigerate in an air-tight container. This can be made well in advance, as it stores quite well. Reheat carefully before serving with the duck. Makes 2½ cups catsup.

*Marionberries may be replaced with blackberries.

**If you want a thicker puree, strain the berries with a wire mesh strainer instead of a food mill.

◆

PEPPER MIX

1 tablespoon salt
2 teaspoons black peppercorns
6 juniper berries
½ teaspoon thyme
¼ teaspoon sugar

▲▲▲▲

Blend all of the ingredients in a small blender jar until finely ground.

CHICKEN in PHYLLO

We developed two fillings for the chicken—liked them equally well—so we included both.

◆◆◆

6 sheets phyllo dough
1-2 tablespoons minced fresh parsley
1-2 tablespoons grated Parmesan cheese
olive oil spray
3 whole chicken breasts,
    skinned, boned, and cut in half

1 recipe Apricot-Mustard and
    Bacon Filling
        or
1 recipe Shrimp, Cilantro, and
    Anaheim Pepper Filling

▲▲▲▲

Prepare the filling of your choice.
    Preheat oven to 375°.
    Lay one sheet of phyllo on a clean work surface, with the long side facing you. Spray with olive oil, and sprinkle with a bit of parsley and Parmesan. Fold in half so the two short edges meet.
    Divide the filling among the six sheets of phyllo, placing the filling a fourth of the way down from the top edge of the phyllo. Cover with a chicken breast half. Fold down the top of the dough over the chicken breast and fold in the sides. Roll up, spraying the final fold so it will seal.
    Place on an ungreased baking sheet. Continue with the remainder of the filling and chicken breasts. Spray the tops of all the phyllo rolls. Bake 20 minutes.

◆

APRICOT-MUSTARD and BACON FILLING

8 strips thickly sliced bacon
1/4 cup Apricot Mustard (see Glossary)
1/4 cup mayonnaise
1/4 cup minced fresh parsley

▲▲▲▲

Cook the bacon until crisp. Drain and mince.
    Combine the minced bacon and remaining ingredients, mixing well. Makes topping for 1 recipe of Chicken in Phyllo, serving 6.

◆

SHRIMP, CILANTRO, and ANAHEIM PEPPER FILLING

2 cloves garlic, minced
8 ounces medium shrimp,
    peeled and deveined
4 teaspoons minced fresh cilantro
4 teaspoons minced fresh
    Anaheim pepper
1/4 cup mayonnaise

▲▲▲▲

Sauté the garlic and shrimp in a nonstick skillet until the shrimp turn pink. Set aside to cool. When cool, chop the shrimp. Combine the shrimp, cilantro, Anaheim pepper, and mayonnaise. Makes topping for 1 recipe of Chicken in Phyllo, serving 6.

GRILLED LAMB CHOPS with PINOT NOIR SAUCE

Once the sauce is underway, these lamb chops are a "quick finish" for a dinner—and an excellent complement to Pinot Noir.

◆◆◆

1 recipe Pinot Noir Sauce (recipe follows)

◆

LAMB CHOPS

12 lamb chops, 1" thick
salt
black pepper
garlic powder
dried rosemary leaves
2 tablespoons minced fresh parsley

▲▲▲▲

Prepare the barbecue grill.

Trim any excess fat from the lamb chops. Sprinkle the chops with salt, pepper, garlic powder, and rosemary. When the grill is ready, cook the lamb chops 4 minutes per side for medium rare. Place a spoonful of Pinot Noir sauce on each dinner plate. Arrange 2-3 chops per person on each plate. Garnish with the minced parsley. Serves 4-6.

◆

PINOT NOIR SAUCE

3 tablespoons butter
10 ounces onions, coarsely chopped
2 cups Pinot Noir
1½ cups lamb or chicken stock
½ cup demi-glace*
½ cup heavy cream
2 tablespoons butter
salt to taste
black pepper to taste

▲▲▲▲

Melt the butter in a heavy saucepan, and add the onions. Sauté, stirring frequently, until the onions are very soft and just barely turning brown (about 20 minutes).

Remove from the heat and puree. Yields about ¾ cup puree.

Return the onion puree to the heavy saucepan. Add the Pinot Noir and reduce volume by half over medium high heat. Add the stock and demi-glace. Reduce by half again. Add the cream, reducing by a fourth. Whisk in the butter. Add salt and pepper to taste. Set aside.

(Keep warm if you plan to use immediately. Otherwise, refrigerate until ready to use, then gently reheat.) Makes about 1½ cups sauce.

*The Joy of Cooking *offers a recipe for demi-glace.*

TOMATO-GARLIC FRENCH BREAD

This is a great way to "freshen up" the taste of day-old French bread and is particularly nice with fish or grilled meats.

◆◆◆

1 loaf good-quality French bread
¼ cup chopped and seeded tomato
2 teaspoons minced garlic
4 teaspoons olive oil
sprinkling of salt
⅓ cup finely grated Jarlsberg cheese

▲▲▲▲

Preheat oven to 350°.

Cut the loaf of bread in half lengthwise. Set aside.

Combine the tomato, garlic, and olive oil in a small blender jar and blend. Add a bit of salt. Spread the mixture on the French bread halves and top with the grated cheese.

Heat in the oven about 8-10 minutes, until the bread is heated through, and cheese melts.

WILD RICE PANCAKES

These are often our first choice to accompany the Peppered Duck Breast (recipe page 94). They also work well with the Spicy Turkey Breast (receipe page 99) or served with maple syrup for brunch.

◆◆◆

$2/3$ cup chicken stock
6 tablespoons couscous
3 cups cooked Wild Rice (recipe follows)
$3/4$ cup minced onion
1 tablespoon flour
1 teaspoon salt
$1/4$ teaspoon black pepper
3 eggs
1 tablespoon olive oil
$1 1/2$ teaspoons hot chili oil

▲▲▲▲

Bring the stock to a boil. Stir in the couscous and return to a boil; then remove from the heat, cover, and set aside for 5 minutes. After 5 minutes, uncover and fluff with a fork. Set aside to cool.

Combine the cooked Wild Rice, minced onion, flour, salt, and pepper, mixing well. Lightly beat the eggs and add to the Wild Rice along with the cooked couscous. Makes about 4 cups.

Combine the olive and hot chili oils. Brush a nonstick skillet with the oil mixture. Using a $1/4$-cup measure, place batter for 4 pancakes in the skillet, flattening the mixture with the back side of a spatula. Cook over medium heat until the pancake is firmed up and nicely browned, about 5 minutes. Turn and cook the other side three minutes.

Continue with the remaining batter, oiling the pan as necessary. (You can hold the already cooked pancakes in a warmed oven.) Makes 12 pancakes, serving 4-6.

◆

WILD RICE

1 tablespoon olive oil
$1/4$ cup minced shallots
2 cups wild rice
3 cups stock

▲▲▲▲

Using a small stock pot, sauté the shallots in the olive oil. Add the wild rice and cook for 2 minutes, stirring constantly. Add the stock, cover, and simmer 45 minutes.

Use this as the base for Wild Rice Pancakes or the beginning of a seasoned wild rice. It keeps well in the refrigerator.

Makes 6 cups cooked Wild Rice.

CORN and JALAPEÑO CAKES with ROASTED RED PEPPER SAUCE

We frequently serve these flavorful corn cakes with fresh red snapper or halibut.

◆◆◆

1 recipe Roasted Red Pepper Sauce
   (recipe follows)
3-4 tablespoons minced fresh cilantro

◆

PANCAKES

½ cup boiling water
¼ cup cornmeal
1½-2 cups corn kernels, fresh or frozen
3 tablespoons finely minced
   fresh jalapeño pepper
2 tablespoons finely minced onion
2 eggs
¼ cup nonfat yogurt
½ cup flour
2 tablespoons melted butter
½ teaspoon salt
1 teaspoon sugar
½ teaspoon baking powder
½ teaspoon baking soda
olive oil for cooking

▲▲▲▲

Pour the boiling water over the cornmeal and set aside.

Combine the corn, jalapeño, and onion in a mixing bowl. Set aside.

Combine the eggs, yogurt, flour, melted butter, salt, sugar, baking powder, and baking soda in a blender jar along with the cornmeal mixture. Blend to liquefy. Pour into the mixing bowl along with the corn, mixing well.

Brush a nonstick skillet with a small amount of olive oil. Using a fourth-cup measure, cook in small batches over medium heat, 3 minutes per side. Makes 12 pancakes. Serve with the Roasted Red Pepper Sauce and garnish with the fresh cilantro. Serves 4-6.

◆

ROASTED RED PEPPER SAUCE

2 tablespoons butter
2-3 teaspoons minced fresh garlic
½ cup minced canned red pepper
2 tablespoons flour
¾ cup vegetable or chicken broth

▲▲▲▲

Melt the butter. Add the garlic, and sauté briefly until softened but not brown. Add the red pepper, and cook an additional minute. Sprinkle with the flour, and stir to incorporate. Add the broth. Simmer until thickened and there is no raw flour taste. May be made ahead and reheated.

SPICY TURKEY BREAST *with* ORANGE *and* ROSEMARY

This is a low-calorie dinner entrée. Any leftovers are wonderful in sandwiches or on a salad such as the Turkey Nectarine Salad (recipe page 67).

◆◆◆

2 tablespoons butter or margarine
2 tablespoons flour

4 large shallots, minced
$^1/_2$ cup low salt soy sauce
$^1/_2$ cup orange juice (fresh squeezed best)
2 tablespoons olive oil
$^1/_4$ cup chopped fresh rosemary
   or 4 teaspoons dried leaves, crumbled
$^1/_4$ cup rice wine vinegar
2 tablespoons orange zest
2 tablespoons honey
$^1/_4$ teaspoon dried red chilies
1 tablespoon hot chili oil

1 3-4 pound boneless turkey breast half, skinned

Garnish:
   orange slices
   parsley

▲▲▲▲

Thoroughly blend butter and flour. Set aside.
   Combine the next ten ingredients and place in a nonreactive bowl or a ziplock bag.

Separate the small tenderloin from the turkey breast. Place the turkey breast between 2 sheets of plastic wrap. Flatten to uniform thickness. Repeat with the tenderloin. Place the turkey pieces in marinade. Cover and seal tightly. Refrigerate 4-6 hours, or overnight, turning the meat in the marinade occasionally.

Reserving the marinade, remove the turkey and place the breast on a rack set in a shallow baking pan. (Set aside the small tenderloin.)

Pour $^1/_2$″ hot water into the baking pan and set in a preheated 375° oven. Bake 45 minutes, turning and basting the turkey every 15 minutes with marinade. Add the reserved tenderloin for the last 20 minutes of baking.

Strain the reserved marinade into a non-reactive saucepan. Heat to a simmer. Whisk in the flour/butter mixture, cooking just enough to lightly thicken. Set aside and keep warm.

Slice the turkey across the grain and place on a warmed platter. Nap with sauce. Garnish with orange slices and parsley. Serves 6-8.

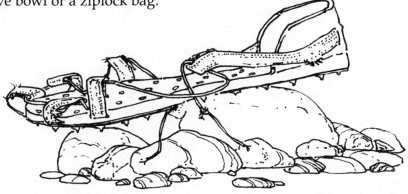

BARBECUED TROUT *with* ONION-CAPER RELISH

A great summer entrée—this is just as much fun to eat as it is to make!

◆◆◆

1 recipe Onion-Caper Relish
    (recipe follows)

◆

TROUT

4 whole, boneless trout, 8-10 ounces each
$1/2$ cup olive oil
$1/4$ cup lemon juice
1 tablespoon minced onion
1 clove garlic, minced
$1/4$ teaspoon salt
$1/4$ teaspoon black pepper
1 teaspoon dill weed
1 teaspoon sugar

▲▲▲▲

Remove the heads from the trout. Place the trout in a noncorrosive dish. Whisk together the olive oil, lemon juice, onion, garlic, salt, pepper, dill weed, and sugar. Pour over the trout. Marinate 2 hours.

Prepare the barbecue grill. When ready, place the trout, skin side down, on tinfoil on the grill. Barbecue 8-10 minutes, until the meat flakes easily with a fork. Remove from the grill, and garnish with Onion-Caper Relish. Serve immediately. Serves 6-8.

◆

ONION-CAPER RELISH

1 tablespoon olive oil
$1/2$ cup chopped yellow onion
$1/2$ cup chopped red onion
$1/2$ cup chopped red pepper
1 clove garlic, minced
$1/2$ teaspoon finely minced lemon zest
1 tablespoon drained capers
1 tablespoon tomato paste
2 tablespoons minced fresh parsley
salt to taste
black pepper to taste

▲▲▲▲

Heat the olive oil in a skillet. Add the onions, red pepper, and garlic. Sauté 5 minutes, over medium heat, stirring constantly. Add the lemon zest, capers, tomato paste, and parsley, mixing well. Cook another 2 minutes. Season to taste with salt and pepper. Set aside.

Rewarm when ready to use. (This may be prepared up to 2 days in advance.) If you prepare it ahead, cover well and refrigerate.

SCALLOPS *in* ONION-WINE SAUCE

We often serve this with angel hair pasta and a crisp green salad.

¹/₄ cup flour
¹/₄ cup grated Parmesan cheese
1 tablespoon ground dry basil leaves
dash of cayenne
¹/₄ teaspoon salt
¹/₈ teaspoon black pepper
3 tablespoon butter
2 onions, thinly sliced
1 tablespoon flour
¹/₂ cup white wine*
1 cup clam juice
2 pounds scallops
1 teaspoon wine vinegar

▲▲▲▲

Combine flour, Parmesan, basil, cayenne, salt, and pepper. Set aside.

Melt 1 tablespoon of the butter in a heavy saucepan, and lightly brown the onions in the butter. Sprinkle the flour over the onions and cook until the flour starts to brown. Add the wine and clam juice. Simmer 15 minutes.

While the onions are simmering, dredge scallops lightly in the flour mixture, shaking off excess.

Melt the remaining 2 tablespoons butter in a skillet. Sauté the scallops 3 minutes on each side. Add to the onion mixture along with the wine vinegar, mixing well. Simmer over low heat for 3-5 minutes. The sauce should thicken slightly. Season with salt and pepper to taste.

Do not use a high acid wine to prepare this dish.

BASIL GREEN BEANS

Now that we are able to purchase high-quality, whole, frozen green beans locally, we keep them on hand for those surprise winter guests. Someone will invariably ask us how we are able to get such fresh green beans in the middle of winter!

◆◆◆

1 pound frozen green beans
1 tablespoon butter
1 tablespoon olive oil
1 cup thinly sliced onion
1 large clove garlic, minced
1 tablespoon dry basil leaves
¹/₄ cup chicken stock
¹/₂ cup red pepper slices
salt to taste
black pepper to taste

▲▲▲▲

Place the green beans in a colander, and run under water to remove ice crystals. Set aside.

Heat the butter and olive oil in a large, nonstick skillet over medium low heat. Add the onion and garlic, tossing to coat well. Cook until the onion is softened, about 10 minutes.

Add the basil and stock, and continue to cook until most of the liquid has evaporated. Add the green beans and red pepper slices. Continue to cook until the beans are cooked through, 5-8 minutes. Season with salt and pepper to taste.

Serve immediately. Serves 6-8.

MASHED POTATOES *with* ROASTED GARLIC, BASIL, *and* SUN-DRIED TOMATOES

Delicious? Absolutely! Leftovers are a great base for a potato soup, or can be formed into patties, dipped in cornmeal, and sautéed for breakfast.

◆◆◆

2 pounds baking potatoes
2 tablespoons snipped
   sun-dried tomatoes
¼ cup butter
¼ cup minced fresh basil
1 tablespoon mashed roasted garlic
   (see Glossary)
4-6 tablespoons half and half
½ teaspoon salt
½ teaspoon black pepper

▲▲▲▲

Boil the potatoes in lightly salted water until they are tender.

Cover the tomatoes with hot water to soften. When soft, drain and set aside.

When the potatoes are cooked, drain and transfer to a mixing bowl. Add the softened, drained tomatoes, butter, basil, and roasted garlic. Beat to mix together. Add 4 tablespoons half and half, salt, and pepper. Add the additional half and half if the potatoes seem dry. Serve immediately. Serves 6-8.

BEET GREENS *and* MUSHROOMS

If fresh beet greens are unavailable, fresh spinach may be substituted, but you should try it with fresh beet greens at least once!

◆◆◆

1 tablespoon butter
2 tablespoons olive oil
½ cup minced onion
1 clove garlic, minced
8 ounces mushrooms,
   stemmed and sliced
6 cups stemmed and washed
   beet greens
salt to taste
black pepper to taste
splash of balsamic vinegar (optional)

▲▲▲▲

Heat the butter and olive oil in a nonstick pan. Add the onion and garlic, sautéeing 2 minutes over medium heat. Add the mushrooms and cook 5-8 minutes, until they are softened.

Add the beet greens and toss to combine. Cook until the beet greens are wilted, stirring frequently. Add salt and pepper to taste. Add a splash of balsamic vinegar. Serves 4-6.

OVEN ROASTED or BARBECUED CHICKEN

The marinade for this dish provides a moist, finished product. Oven-roasting, barbecuing, or barbecue-smoking this chicken works well—any leftovers are a great beginning for smoked chicken salad.

◆◆◆

1 whole chicken (3-3½ pounds),
   cut in half
½ cup low salt soy sauce
1 tablespoon Tabasco sauce
½ lemon, sliced
1 clove garlic, slivered
1 green onion, sliced
2 tablespoons brown sugar

▲▲▲▲

Place the chicken halves in a large ziplock bag. Combine the remaining ingredients and pour over the chicken. Seal, releasing any air from the bag, and refrigerate overnight, turning occasionally.

Preheat oven to 375° or prepare a barbecue.

Remove the chicken from the marinade, reserving the lemon slices. Place the lemon slices in a baking dish or on the barbecue grill and cover with the chicken half, skin side up. Bake or barbecue 40-45 minutes, (or barbecue smoke*) until the juices no longer run pink when the meat is pierced with a fork. Serves 4-6.

*See Glossary for barbecue smoking instructions.

BRINED and BARBECUED LEG of LAMB

The leg of lamb needs to be in the brine for 3 days, so there are no last-minute preparations— you just need to put the lamb on the barbecue.

◆◆◆

1 boned leg of lamb (about 4-5 pounds)
2 quarts water
2 tablespoons dried whole rosemary
2 tablespoons cumin seed
1 tablespoon whole peppercorns
5 cloves garlic, peeled and smashed
½ cup sugar
3 tablespoons salt

▲▲▲▲

Combine all the ingredients, except the leg of lamb, in a saucepan and bring to a boil. Remove from the heat and set aside to cool.

If the leg of lamb is rolled, untie the leg. Trim off any excess fat and leave the leg unrolled.

Place a 2-gallon (or larger) heavy, plastic bag in a baking pan. Put the leg of lamb in the bag. Pour in the cooled brine, squeeze out any air, and tie to seal. Refrigerate 3 days, turning occasionally.

Prepare the barbecue. When the barbecue is ready, remove the leg of lamb from the brine. Discard the brine. Place the leg on the grill and cook, turning occasionally, for about 45 minutes for rare to medium rare. Serves 8.

Optional suggestion: Shiitake Mushroom Bread (recipe page 79), Onion Marmalade (recipe page 60), and this Brined and Barbecued Leg of Lamb make a wonderful sandwich.

PORCINI MUSHROOM RISOTTO

The dried porcini mushrooms and Arborio rice can be found in specialty food stores. It is worth searching them out for this creamy rice dish.

◆◆◆

1 1/2 ounces dried porcini mushrooms
1 1/2 cups boiling water
1/2 cup butter
1/3 cup minced shallots
2 cloves garlic, minced
2 cups Arborio rice
1 teaspoon dried thyme leaves
1 1/4 cups water
5-6 cups chicken stock*
1/4 cup minced fresh parsley

▲▲▲▲

Pour the boiling water over the mushrooms and set aside for 30-45 minutes to allow them to soften. When soft, drain the mushrooms, reserving the soaking liquid. Mince the mushrooms and set aside. Strain the soaking liquid through cheesecloth to remove the grit. (This is an important step; otherwise, the finished product will have a granular texture.) Bring the stock to a low simmer in a small saucepan.

Melt 6 tablespoons of the butter in a heavy-bottomed stock pot. Add the shallots and garlic and sauté 3 minutes, stirring constantly. Add the rice and cook, stirring constantly, until the rice starts to brown.

Add the reserved soaking liquid with additional water to measure 1 1/2 cups. Cook, stirring frequently, over medium heat until most of the liquid has been absorbed. Throughout the cooking process, you will want to maintain the rice mixture at a medium-low simmer.

Add 1 1/4 cups water, minced mushrooms, and thyme. Continue to cook, stirring occasionally, until the liquid is nearly absorbed. Add 1 cup of the simmering stock and reduce, stirring occasionally. Continue with remaining stock, using about 5-6 cups, until the rice is creamy but still has some texture when chewed. The entire process may take half an hour. The final product should be creamy, and the rice should still be a bit firm. Toss in the parsley. (If overcooked, the risotto will turn into a pot of mush!) Serves 6.

This can be prepared with canned chicken stock.

SESAME CORN

This works well with either fresh or frozen corn, making something special of an old standby.

◆◆◆

1 tablespoon sesame oil
1 teaspoon butter
1/3 cup finely minced onion
2 cups corn kernels
2 tablespoons minced fresh parsley
1-2 tablespoons toasted sesame seeds
salt to taste
black pepper to taste

▲▲▲▲

Heat the sesame oil and butter in a skillet. Add the onion and sauté until the onion starts to soften. Add the corn. Stir and cook 5 more minutes. Toss in the parsley and the toasted sesame seeds. Season to taste with salt and pepper. Serves 6-8.

ONION and PEPPER BACON POTATOES

These work well as either a dinner or a brunch side dish. Feel free to substitute regular bacon if you are unable to find pepper bacon.

◆◆◆

½ pound pepper bacon (½" pieces)
2 cups onion, chopped
1 tablespoon olive oil
2 pounds red potatoes, ½" cubes
1½-2 teaspoons finely minced
   fresh rosemary
salt to taste
black pepper to taste

▲▲▲▲

Preheat oven to 375-400°.

Cook the bacon until crisp. Leaving 1 tablespoon of fat in the skillet, drain the bacon and set aside.

Cook chopped onions in the reserved tablespoon of bacon fat. When they have softened, turn out onto a baking sheet. Return the pan to the heat and add the tablespoon of olive oil. Add the potatoes. Cook, stirring frequently until they have started to brown. About 10-15 minutes. Turn out onto the baking sheet with the onions. Add the crisp bacon and mix well. Bake 30 minutes. Remove from the oven, add the rosemary, salt, and pepper. Serves 6-8.

SPICY LAMB MEATLOAF

This spicy loaf also works well with either ground turkey or chicken.

◆◆◆

2 tablespoons butter
1 cup minced onions
½ cup minced celery
2 cloves garlic, minced
1 tablespoon Worcestershire sauce
1 teaspoon ground cumin
2 teaspoons salt
½ teaspoon nutmeg
1-2 tablespoons Chili Garlic Sauce
   (see Glossary)
1 bay leaf
½ cup evaporated milk
½ cup catsup
2 pounds ground lamb
2 eggs
1 cup dry bread crumbs

▲▲▲▲

Preheat oven to 350°.

Melt the butter in a large skillet. Sauté the onions, celery, and garlic 2-3 minutes. Add the Worcestershire, cumin, salt, nutmeg, Chili Garlic Sauce, and bay leaf, sautéeing briefly. Add evaporated milk and catsup. Continue to cook another 2-3 minutes. Remove from the heat. Remove the bay leaf and cool.

Combine the ground lamb, eggs, and bread crumbs. Add the cooled onion mixture, mixing well. Bake in 1 large or 3 small bread pans.

Bake 50-60 minutes in a large pan or 30-40 minutes in a small pan. Serves 8.

BULGUR *with* DRIED CRANBERRIES

A hearty and unusual winter dish that combines nicely with duck, lamb, or beef.

◆◆◆

2 tablespoons olive oil, divided
1 cup chopped onion, divided
4½ cups chicken stock, divided
½ cup dried cranberries
1 cup chopped celery
1 cup sliced mushrooms
2 cups bulgur
½ teaspoon dried oregano leaves
1 teaspoon salt
½ teaspoon black pepper
2 tablespoons minced fresh parsley

▲▲▲▲

Heat 1 tablespoon of the olive oil in a small skillet. Add half of the onions and sauté 2 minutes. Add ½ cup of the stock and the dried cranberries. Sauté until the stock has been absorbed. Set aside.

Heat the remaining tablespoon of olive oil in a stock pot. Add the remaining onion, celery, and mushrooms, sautéeing briefly. Add the bulgur. Cook, stirring constantly, until the bulgur starts to turn golden. Add the reserved cranberry mixture, remaining stock, oregano, salt, and pepper, mixing well. Bring to a boil. Reduce the heat, cover, and cook 15 minutes, at a low simmer. Stir in the parsley, and taste for seasonings. Serves 6-8.

BOBBY'S FRESH GINGER, LEMON, *and* HONEY YAMS

Bobette Moyers, a long-time river resident and one of Steamboat Inn's evening dinner cooks, developed these tasty yams for Jim Van Loan.

2 pounds medium-sized yams
   or sweet potatoes
      peeled, cut in ½"-thick slices
1 tablespoon lemon zest
4 teaspoons minced fresh ginger
3 tablespoons honey
salt to taste
black pepper to taste
2 tablespoons butter, melted

▲▲▲▲

Parboil the yams in lightly salted water until crisp-tender. Do not overcook. Drain well.

Preheat oven to 375°.

Lightly butter a 9" × 9" baking dish. Place a layer of yams in the dish and sprinkle with lemon zest and ginger, and drizzle with honey. Lightly salt and pepper the layer. Continue layering until all the ingredients are used. Bake 20 minutes. Remove from the oven and toss with the melted butter. Serves 6-8.

BUTTERNUT SQUASH with ONION and FRESH ROSEMARY

This will be a welcome dish for those of you who always plant way too many squash plants in your summer garden! This recipe will also convert those who "think" they do not like squash.

◆◆◆

8 cups butternut squash, ½" cubes
   (about 1 small squash)
¼ cup butter
2 cups thinly sliced onion
2 tablespoons minced fresh parsley
1 tablespoon finely minced
   fresh rosemary
¼ teaspoon salt
¼ teaspoon black pepper

▲▲▲▲

Bring a pot of lightly salted water to a boil. Add the cubed squash. Return to a boil and cook 10-15 minutes, until the squash is crisp-tender. (Do not overcook or it will be too mushy.) Drain and set aside.

Melt the butter in a large sauté pan. Add the onions and cook over medium heat, until they are soft but not brown. Add the parsley and rosemary, stirring well. Add the butternut squash, and toss gently to combine. Add the salt and pepper. Cook 2-3 minutes until the squash is heated through. Serves 6-8.

SPINACH and FRESH BEETS

Beet greens, mustard greens, or chard work well as a substitute for the spinach.

◆◆◆

2 large fresh beets,
   cooked and cut into julienne*

2 tablespoons olive oil
2 cloves garlic, minced
1 bunch fresh spinach
   (7-8 cups shredded)
salt to taste
black pepper to taste

▲▲▲▲

Heat the olive oil in a large sauté pan over medium heat. Add the garlic. Cook, stirring constantly, until the garlic just starts to brown.

Add the beets and continue to cook, stirring constantly for 3-4 minutes.

When the beets are hot, add the spinach and cook until the spinach wilts, 2-3 minutes.

Season with salt and pepper. Serves 4.

To cook the beets, cut off the tops. Then place the beets in a stock pot and cover with water. Boil for 30-40 minutes until they are tender, but still a bit crisp, when you pierce them with a fork.

GRILLED EGGPLANT *and* SQUASH *with* RED PEPPER MAYONNAISE

Try a spash of balsamic vinegar in place of the mayonnaise, or serve as an hors d'oeuvre with roasted garlic and French bread.

◆◆◆

1 recipe Red Pepper Mayonnaise
  (recipe follows)

2 small eggplant
2 small zucchini squash
2 small yellow squash
salt to taste
black pepper to taste
olive oil

▲▲▲▲

Cut the eggplant lengthwise into ½" wide slices. Cut the zucchini and yellow squash lengthwise into ¼-½" wide slices.

Place the vegetables on a paper-lined baking tray and sprinkle with salt. Let set for 30 minutes.

While the vegetables are setting, prepare the Red Pepper Mayonnaise.

Prepare the barbecue grill. When the grill is ready, wipe the excess salt and moisture from the vegetables. Lightly oil the grill, or spray with olive oil spray. Place the vegetables on the grill.

Brush the vegetables with olive oil, and sprinkle with salt and pepper. Cook 4 to 5 minutes per side, occasionally brushing with olive oil, until they are nicely browned and cooked through. Serve with the Red Pepper Mayonnaise. Serves 4-6.

◆

RED PEPPER MAYONNAISE

1 cup mayonnaise
2 cloves roasted garlic
¼ cup minced roasted red pepper
  (see Glossary)

▲▲▲▲

Combine the mayonnaise, garlic, and red pepper, mixing well. Cover and refrigerate until ready to use.

NAPA CABBAGE and CORN SALAD

This recipe is another creation from Pat's trip to Japan. Our friend, Yoko, says we don't have quite the right ingredients, but it is acceptable!

◆◆◆

1 recipe Dressing (recipe follows)

2 cups shredded spinach

5 cups Napa cabbage, thinly sliced
1 cup cooked corn, fresh or frozen
$\frac{1}{2}$ cup diagonally cut green onion tops
1 sheet dried seaweed, cut in
    $\frac{1}{4}'' \times 1''$ strips (see Glossary)
2 tablespoons black sesame seeds

▲▲▲▲

Set out 6 salad plates. Arrange the shredded spinach around the rim of the plates.

Combine the Napa cabbage, corn, green onions, and seaweed strips, tossing well. Toss with enough Dressing to coat the cabbage.

Divide the cabbage mixture among the salad plates. Top with the sesame seeds and serve. Serves 6.

◆

DRESSING

$\frac{1}{3}$ cup rice vinegar
$\frac{1}{4}$ cup vegetable oil
2 tablespoons sesame oil
3 tablespoons low salt soy sauce
1 large clove garlic, minced
2 teaspoons minced fresh ginger

▲▲▲▲

Combine the dressing ingredients. Set aside.

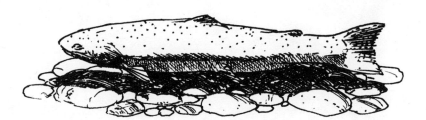

POTATO GRATIN *with* FRESH SPINACH *and* MUSHROOMS

A variation of scalloped potatoes—
any leftovers are a great beginning for a potato soup.

◆◆◆

1 10" pie plate, buttered

2 tablespoons olive oil
¹/₃ cup minced shallots
2 cups lightly packed sliced
    fresh spinach,
1 teaspoon Worcestershire sauce
¹/₂ pound mushrooms, cleaned and sliced
1 tablespoon minced garlic
1 pound red potatoes, thinly sliced
salt to taste
black pepper to taste

3 tablespoons grated Swiss cheese
1 cup chicken stock

▲▲▲▲

Preheat the oven to 350°.

Heat 1 tablespoon olive oil in a skillet. Add the shallots and spinach and cook just until the spinach is wilted. Remove from the heat.

Heat the remaining 1 tablespoon olive oil. Add the Worcestershire sauce, mushrooms, and garlic. Cook until the mushrooms just start to exude their juices. Remove from the heat.

Cover the bottom of the buttered dish with a layer of sliced potatoes. Lightly salt and pepper. Cover with two more layers of potatoes. Spread the spinach out in a layer. Cover with a layer of potatoes. Salt and pepper the layer. Add another layer of potatoes and then the mushrooms. Layer the remaining potatoes. Top with the grated cheese. Pour the stock over the potatoes. Bake 45 minutes to 1 hour.

Let the gratin set 5 minutes before cutting. Cut into wedges and serve. Serves 6-8.

Desserts

◆ ◆ ◆

TOASTED COCONUT CAKE
with **TOASTED COCONUT-PECAN FILLING**

CHOCOLATE FILBERT TORTE

SESAME GINGER WAFERS

FROZEN ORANGE MOUSSE
with **FRESH BLACKBERRIES**

COCONUT CORNMEAL WAFERS

STEAMBOAT INN CREAM PIE FILLING

PECAN *and* **FRESH GINGER TART**
with **CORNMEAL CRUST**

DRIED CRANBERRY *and* **SOUR CREAM TART**

RASPBERRY TART

TOASTED NUT LACE COOKIES

STEAMBOAT COOKIES

PEARS *with* **CRYSTALLIZED GINGER**

TOASTED ALMOND CAKE *with*
CARAMELIZED PEAR FILLING *and* **CHOCOLATE GLAZE**

CREAM PUFFS *with* **CARAMELIZED PEAR FILLING**
and **CHOCOLATE GLAZE**

FILBERT ROULADE *with* **COFFEE CREAM FILLING**

STEAMBOAT INN'S FRUIT PIES

BROILED PEARS *with* **LIME SAUCE**

GINGER SORBET

APPLE CINNAMON TORTE

ORANGE WALNUT CAKE

DRIED PEAR *and* **WALNUT BISCOTTI**

ALMOND BUTTER BARS

BUTTERMILK POPPY SEED CAKE

TOASTED COCONUT CAKE with TOASTED COCONUT-PECAN FILLING

If you are craving coconut, this cake is the perfect dessert for you!

◆◆◆

1 recipe Toasted Coconut-Pecan Filling
   (recipe follows)

◆

CAKE

3 cups sweetened flake coconut
1½ cups sifted cake flour
2½ teaspoons baking powder
½ teaspoon salt
¼ teaspoon baking soda
½ cup butter, room temperature
1 cup sugar
2 tablespoons lime juice
1 teaspoon coconut extract
¾ cup unsweetened coconut milk
3 tablespoons 2% milk
4 egg whites
lightly sweetened whipped cream
   (optional)

▲▲▲▲

Line two 8" round cake pans with parchment. Butter and flour the pans.

Toast the coconut in a 275° oven until nicely browned. Set aside 1 cup toasted coconut for the filling. Grind the remaining coconut until fine.

Sift the cake flour, baking powder, salt, and baking soda. Stir in the ground coconut.

Cream the butter and sugar. Add the lime juice and coconut extract, mixing well.

Mix together the coconut milk and 2% milk. Add alternately with flour to the creamed butter and sugar mixture.

Beat the egg whites until stiff but not dry. Stir a quarter of the whites into the batter to lighten it. Gently fold in remaining whites. Pour into prepared pans. Bake 20-25 minutes in a preheated 350° oven.

Remove from the oven and turn out onto racks to cool.

To assemble: Lay one cake layer on a serving platter. Spread half of the Toasted Coconut-Pecan Filling on the layer. Top with the second layer. Spread the remaining filling on the top of the cake.* Refrigerate until ready to serve.

*For a fancier presentation, you can frost the sides of the cake with lightly sweetened whipped cream.

◆

TOASTED COCONUT-PECAN FILLING

¾ cup 2% milk
1 teaspoon gelatin
½ cup sugar
2 egg yolks
2 tablespoons butter, room temperature
½ teaspoon coconut extract
1 cup toasted coconut
1 cup toasted pecans, coarsely chopped

▲▲▲▲

Soften the gelatin in the milk.

Combine the gelatin-milk mixture with the sugar, egg yolks, butter, and coconut extract in a small saucepan. Cook, stirring constantly over low heat until the mixture thickens, about 10 minutes. Do not let the mixture boil.

Remove from the heat and stir in the toasted coconut and chopped pecans. Set aside to cool. Makes enough for a 2-layer cake.

CHOCOLATE FILBERT TORTE

We hope you will appreciate this rich dessert. Sharon must have made thirty versions before she was pleased with the final result!

◆◆◆

1 recipe Filbert Layer
   (recipe follows)
1 recipe Chocolate Layer
   (recipe follows)
1 recipe Chocolate Glaze
   (recipe follows)

▲▲▲▲

Cut the Chocolate Layer into two layers. Place one layer on a serving platter and spread with a thin layer of Chocolate Glaze. Top with the Filbert Layer. Spread with a thin layer of the Chocolate Glaze and top with the remaining Chocolate Layer. Glaze the top of the torte with the remaining Chocolate Glaze. Serves 6-8.

◆

FILBERT LAYER

2 round cake pans (9")
3 egg yolks
6 tablespoons sugar, divided
1 teaspoon filbert liqueur
2 tablespoons flour
1/2 teaspoon baking powder
2 egg whites
dash of cream of tartar
6 ounces Filbert Paste (see Glossary)

▲▲▲▲

Preheat oven to 350°.

Grease and line the cake pans with parchment or waxed paper. Butter and flour the paper, tapping out any excess flour. Reserve one pan for the chocolate layer.

Beat the egg yolks until fluffy. Gradually add 3 tablespoons of the sugar and continue to beat until thick and lemon colored. Add the flour, liqueur, and baking powder and beat just long enough to combine.

Beat the egg whites with the cream of tartar until frothy. Gradually add the remaining 3 tablespoons sugar. Beat until stiff but not dry. Sprinkle the filbert paste over the whites and partially incorporate with 4 quick turns. Add yolk mixture and gently fold to incorporate.

Pour into the prepared pan and bake for 40-45 minutes in a hot water bath. When baked, transfer to a rack to cool, removing the baking paper.

◆

CHOCOLATE LAYER

3 ounces unsweetened chocolate
6 tablespoons butter
1/4 cup water
3 eggs, separated
1 teaspoon filbert liqueur
1/2 cup sugar
1/4 cup Filbert Paste (see Glossary)
1/2 cup sifted flour

▲▲▲▲

Combine the chocolate, butter, and water in the top of a double boiler. Melt over simmering water. When melted, remove from the heat and cool slightly.

Beat together the egg yolks, filbert liquor, and sugar until thickened. Add the melted chocolate and filbert paste, mixing well. Add the flour, blending thoroughly.

Beat the egg whites until stiff but not dry. Stir a fourth of the whites into the batter to lighten it. Gently fold in remaining whites.

Pour into the prepared baking pan. Bake in a water bath 30-35 minutes. Remove from the oven and cool before serving. Serves 8.

◆

CHOCOLATE GLAZE

4 ounces bittersweet chocolate,
    broken into chunks
2 tablespoons hot coffee
1 tablespoon butter

▲▲▲▲

Microwave the chocolate and coffee in a glass measuring cup 30-40 seconds or until about half of the chocolate is melted. Remove from the microwave.

Stir until all of the chocolate has melted. Add the butter and continue to stir until well blended and smooth.

SESAME GINGER WAFERS

Quick and simple to make! The dough freezes well, so they are easy to keep on hand.

◆◆◆

2 cups flour
$^1/_2$ teaspoon baking soda
$^1/_2$ teaspoon salt
1 cup butter or margarine,
    room temperature
$^3/_4$ cup sugar
1 egg
3 tablespoons snipped candied ginger
$^1/_2$ teaspoon sesame oil
$^1/_3$ cup toasted sesame seeds

▲▲▲▲

Sift the flour, baking soda, and salt together.

Cream the butter and sugar. Add the egg, candied ginger, sesame oil, and sesame seeds, mixing well. Add the sifted ingredients.

Refrigerate the dough for an hour or more, or freeze for later use.

Preheat oven to 350°.

Pinch off enough dough to form 1" balls. Place the balls of dough on an ungreased cookie sheet. Bake in a preheated oven 8-10 minutes, until lightly browned. Makes about 30 cookies.

FROZEN ORANGE MOUSSE *with* FRESH BLACKBERRIES

Blueberries, fresh or candied orange slices, or strawberries will work well as a topping if blackberries happen to be out of season.

◆◆◆

3/4 cup sugar
2 tablespoons minced orange zest
1/3 cup water
6 egg yolks
3/4 cup nonfat plain yogurt
3/4 cup nonfat vanilla yogurt
1 cup whipping cream
1 tablespoon orange liqueur
3-4 cups fresh ripe blackberries

▲▲▲▲

Process the sugar and zest in a processor until they are well combined. Transfer the orange-sugar mixture to a nonreactive saucepan and add the water. Heat until the sugar dissolves; then boil rapidly 5 minutes. Remove from the heat and set aside.

Beat the egg yolks in a large mixing bowl until thick and light in color. With the machine running, slowly add orange syrup. Beat until the mixture has thickened and cooled. Gently stir in the plain and vanilla yogurt.

Whip the cream and liqueur until the cream holds soft peaks. Do not overbeat. Carefully fold the cream into the yogurt mixture.

Ladle the mousse into eight parfait or wine glasses. Cover well and freeze until firm. (May be prepared several days ahead.)

Thirty minutes before serving, transfer the mousse to the refrigerator.

Just prior to serving, mound berries in the top of the dessert glasses and serve. Serves 8.

COCONUT CORNMEAL WAFERS

A rich and crunchy accompaniment to a sorbet or ice cream. Since these are easy to prepare and freeze well, we usually have some on hand. A short time out of the freezer allows them to be cut and baked.

◆◆◆

1/2 pound butter, room temperature
1 cup sugar
2 egg yolks
1/2-3/4 teaspoon coconut extract
1 1/2 cups flour
1 cup cornmeal
1/2 cup flaked coconut

Cream the butter and sugar. Add the egg yolks and coconut extract, mixing well. Add flour, cornmeal, and coconut, blending thoroughly. Form the dough into 2, 1" diameter logs and wrap in plastic wrap. Refrigerate until firm, or freeze the dough, well wrapped.

Preheat oven to 350°.

Slice cookies into 1/4" rounds and bake on an ungreased baking sheet 8-10 minutes. Makes 24-30 cookies.

STEAMBOAT INN CREAM PIE FILLING

This is the base recipe we use for our cream pies. The recipe makes enough filling for 2 pies, and the flavor variations are endless.

◆◆◆

2 9″ prebaked pie shells
1 recipe Crust (recipe page 125)

³/₄ cup cornstarch
2 cups sugar
³/₄ teaspoon salt
6 cups scalded milk
9 eggs
6 tablespoons butter or margarine
1¹/₂ teaspoons vanilla

▲▲▲▲

Combine the cornstarch, sugar, and salt in a heavy saucepan. Stir in the scalded milk. Bring to a boil over medium high heat. Boil 2 minutes. (The mixture will thicken.)

Beat the eggs together. Add a small amount of the hot milk mixture to the eggs. Stir the warmed egg mixture into the thickened milk. Cook 1 minute, stirring constantly.

Remove from the heat and stir in the butter and vanilla.

If you would like two flavors of cream pie, divide the mixture in half and add flavoring to each, while the mixture is still warm.

Makes filling for 2, 9″ cream pies.

To assemble: Pour the filling into a prebaked shell and refrigerate until set, about 2 hours. Top with whipped cream, and garnish with shaved chocolate, toasted coconut, toasted almonds, or chopped peanuts, to indicate the flavoring of the pie. Each pie serves 6-8.

◆

CHOCOLATE CREAM

3 ounces unsweetened chocolate

▲▲▲▲

Add 3 ounces of unsweetened chocolate per each half recipe of warm cream base.

◆

COCONUT CREAM

1 teaspoon coconut extract
1 cup toasted flake coconut

▲▲▲▲

Add 1 teaspoon coconut extract and 1 cup toasted flake coconut per each half recipe of warm cream base.

◆

ALMOND CREAM

1 teaspoon almond extract
1 cup toasted sliced almonds

▲▲▲▲

Add 1 teaspoon almond extract and 1 cup toasted sliced almonds per each half recipe of warm cream base.

◆

PEANUT BUTTER CREAM

¹/₂-³/₄ cup peanut butter
(creamy or crunchy)

▲▲▲▲

Add ¹/₂-³/₄ cup peanut butter to each half recipe of warm cream base. This is a very rich pie.

PECAN *and* FRESH GINGER TART *with* CORNMEAL CRUST

The firm texture of this double-crust tart allows it to be transported for a picnic or to a potluck. When kept at room temperature it holds for a day or two.

◆◆◆

1 9″ × 1″ tart pan with removable bottom

◆

CORNMEAL CRUST

1 cup flour
1/3 cup cornmeal
5 tablespoons sugar
1/4 teaspoon salt
1/2 cup cold butter, cut into 8 pieces
4 tablespoons cold water

▲▲▲▲

Add the flour, cornmeal, sugar, and salt to the work bowl of a food processor. Process briefly to combine. Add the chunks of cold butter and process until the mixture is well combined.

With the machine running, slowly add the cold water. Continue processing until moist clumps form. Remove from the work bowl and form into a ball.*

Divide the dough in half. Form one half into a ball and roll out between 2 lightly floured sheets of plastic wrap. Line the springform pan with the dough. Refrigerate 30 minutes. Cover and set aside the other half of dough.

Preheat oven to 400°.

When the dough-lined pan has chilled, remove from the refrigerator. Line the pan with foil and pie weights. Bake 10 minutes, remove the foil and weights and bake an additional 5 minutes. Remove from the oven and set aside to cool. While the pan is cooling, prepare the filling.

Pour the filling into the crust. Roll out the reserved piece of dough between 2 sheets of lightly floured plastic wrap. Cover the filling and press the dough around the edge of the pan to seal.

Bake in the preheated oven 25-30 minutes. Transfer to a rack to cool. Serves 6-8.

*This recipe makes dough for 1, 9″ × 1″ double-crust tart or 1, 11″ single-crust tart. If using as a prebaked crust, bake in a preheated 375° oven for 15 minutes with foil and pie weights. Remove the weights and foil and bake another 10-15 minutes until lightly browned. Cool before filling.

◆

TOASTED PECAN *and* FRESH GINGER FILLING

5 tablespoons butter
1 tablespoon minced fresh ginger
1 1/4 cups packed brown sugar
2 tablespoons heavy cream
1 tablespoon flour
2 large eggs, lightly beaten
1 1/2 cups toasted pecan halves,
  coarsely chopped

▲▲▲▲

Combine the butter, ginger, brown sugar, cream, and flour in a heavy saucepan. Stir constantly, scraping the sides of the pan, over medium heat until the butter is melted and the sugar is dissolved, 5-10 minutes.

Remove from the heat. Stir in the chopped pecans and the lightly beaten eggs, and cool slightly. Pour into the partially baked crust and proceed as stated above.

DRIED CRANBERRY and SOUR CREAM TART

This started out with cherry and sour cream but was not quite right. The next version was dried cranberry with a chocolate cakelike crust, but we missed the mark again. The third time seems just right!

◆◆◆

1 9″ × 1″ tart pan with removable bottom

1 recipe Cornmeal Crust (recipe page 118)
2 teaspoons finely grated orange zest

2 cups dried cranberries
2 tablespoons orange liqueur
3/4 cup hot water

1 1/3 cups sour cream (light or regular)
6 tablespoons sugar
1/2 teaspoon orange liqueur
2 teaspoons finely minced orange zest
1 egg yolk

▲▲▲▲

Combine the cranberries, orange liqueur, and hot water. Set aside until plump and softened, 2 hours or overnight. When plump, drain well, reserving the liquid.*
   Preheat oven to 375°.
   Prepare Cornmeal Crust with the addition of the 2 teaspoons grated orange zest. Line the tart pan with half of the dough and prebake, following the recipe instructions. Reserve the remaining dough for another use. After the crust has baked, reduce the oven to 350°.
   Combine the sour cream, sugar, orange liqueur, minced orange zest, and egg yolk, mixing well.

Spread the cranberries over the partially baked crust. Pour the sour cream mixture over the berries and spread to the edges of the pan. Bake in the preheated 350° oven 45-50 minutes. Serve warm or at room temperature. Serves 6-8.

Variation: Finely chop or sliver 2-3 ounces semisweet chocolate. Sprinkle over the crust just as it is removed from the oven. Let set 2 minutes to melt, then smooth over the crust.

*If you want a glaze on the tart, add 2 teaspoons sugar and 2 teaspoons cornstarch to the reserved soaking liquid. Place in a nonreactive saucepan. Heat, stirring constantly, until the mixture thickens and is no longer opaque. Cool to room temperature. Pour over the tart before serving.

RASPBERRY TART

Although this tart is best when the raspberries are in season, it will add a splash of color to a winter meal when made with frozen raspberries.

◆◆◆

1 11" tart pan with removable bottom

1 recipe Cornmeal Crust, prebaked
    (recipe page 118)

4 cups raspberries, fresh or frozen*
$^1/_2$-1 cup sugar
    (amount depends on berry sweetness)
2-3 tablespoons cornstarch
$^1/_8$ teaspoon salt
dash of nutmeg
whipped cream
2 tablespoons sugar
melted semi sweet chocolate (optional)

▲▲▲▲

Puree and strain 2 cups of the raspberries. Transfer to a nonreactive saucepan. Add the sugar to taste, cornstarch, salt, and nutmeg.

Heat, stirring constantly, until thickened and mixture is no longer opaque. Set aside.

Distribute the remaining 2 cups berries over the prebaked cornmeal crust. Sprinkle with the 2 tablespoons sugar.

Pour the thickened glaze over the berries, covering well. Refrigerate until firm, 1-2 hours. Cut into wedges and serve, garnished with the whipped cream. (It is best served on the day it is made to assure a crisp crust.) Serves 8-10.

For the chocolate: You can shave the chocolate and sprinkle it over the whipped cream or drizzle melted chocolate over the top of the tart and refrigerate 10 minutes until set, then serve.

*If using frozen berries, strain the whole berries for lining the tart. Too much juice softens the crust.

TOASTED NUT LACE COOKIES

Any toasted, finely ground nut works well for these cookies. They are crisp and flavorful to serve on their own, or they can be shaped into a cup and filled with ice cream or sorbet and topped with a sauce. This makes a most elegant dessert!

◆◆◆

$^1/_2$ cup butter
2 tablespoons half and half
$^1/_2$ cup sugar
1 tablespoon flour
$^2/_3$ cup toasted nuts, finely ground
    (pecans, filberts, almonds, walnuts,
      or mixture)

▲▲▲▲

Grease and flour a large baking sheet.

Preheat oven to 375°.

Combine all of the ingredients in a large skillet and cook until the butter is melted and the ingredients are well combined.

Drop by the teaspoonful onto the prepared baking sheet*, spacing 3 inches apart. Bake 6-8 minutes until golden. Remove from the baking sheet and lay over a rolling pin to cool or, for cookie cups, invert over a small bowl to cool. Makes 24 cookies.

*Work with only one baking sheet at a time, as you need to work quickly with these cookies. Once they cool, these are very crisp cookies and cannot be shaped. The first time you prepare them, these cookies may seem difficult, but once you establish a rhythm they are easy and well worth the effort!

STEAMBOAT COOKIES

We have sold these cookies at the front desk as "monster cookies"—each cookie using ¹/₃ cup dough. At that size the recipe only yields 15-18 cookies! Made "normal" size you should get 3-3¹/₂ dozen cookies.

◆◆◆

1 cup butter or margarine,
    room temperature
²/₃ cup white sugar
²/₃ cup brown sugar
2 tablespoons maple syrup
1 teaspoon vanilla
2 eggs
1¹/₂ cups flour
1¹/₂ cups rolled oats
³/₄ cup wheat germ
³/₄ cup coconut
³/₄ cup chopped walnuts
¹/₄ cup millet
1 teaspoon baking powder
¹/₂ teaspoon baking soda
¹/₂ teaspoon salt
¹/₂ cup chocolate chips

▲▲▲▲

Preheat oven to 350°.

Cream the butter and sugars. Add the maple syrup, vanilla, and eggs, mixing well. Combine the next 9 ingredients and add to the creamed mixture. Stir in the chocolate chips.

Drop by the spoonful onto a greased baking sheet. Bake 12-15 minutes.

PEARS *with* CRYSTALLIZED GINGER

Dessert cannot get any easier than this—nor can anything be tastier!

◆◆◆

Per person:

¹/₂ fresh, ripe pear, cored and sliced
1 quarter-size chunk crystallized
    ginger, slivered (see Glossary)

▲▲▲▲

Fan the pear slices on a dessert plate. Sprinkle the slivered ginger over the pear. Garnish with an edible flower such as a purple pansy.

TOASTED ALMOND CAKE *with* CARAMELIZED PEAR FILLING *and* CHOCOLATE GLAZE

Just one of two uses we have designed for the Caramelized Pear Filling. We are sure you will be able to come up with many more! You will want to keep in mind this has a firm texture after it has been refrigerated, so it will transport easily.

◆◆◆

1 15½″ × 10½″ × 1″ jelly roll pan

2 recipes Caramelized Pear Filling
    (recipe page 123)
1 recipe Chocolate Glaze
    (recipe page 123)

◆

CAKE

8 eggs, separated
1¼ cups sugar
2 teaspoons almond extract
1 teaspoon baking powder
½ teaspoon salt
2 cups finely ground
    graham cracker crumbs
3 tablespoons hot water
1 cup finely ground toasted almonds

▲▲▲▲

Prepare the Caramelized Pear Filling and refrigerate until firm. Line a jelly roll pan with parchment or wax paper. Butter and flour the paper.

Preheat oven to 325°.

Beat the egg yolks until thick and lemon-colored. Gradually add the sugar, beating until the mixture thickens, about 5 minutes. Add the almond extract, baking powder, and salt. Beat in the graham cracker crumbs. Stir in the hot water to lighten the mixture. Fold in the ground nuts.

Beat the egg whites until stiff but not dry. Stir a fourth of the whites into the batter to lighten it. Gently fold in the remaining whites. Pour into the prepared pan and bake 20-25 minutes, until a toothpick comes out clean. Invert onto a cotton towel that has been dusted with powdered sugar. Peel off the paper and let cool.

When the cake has cooled, trim the sides. Cut the cake into 3, 5″ wide strips. Cut each of the strips into two layers. You will end up with 6 strips, each about 5″ wide and 10″ long.

To assemble: Place 1 layer of cake on a platter. Top with one-fifth of the Caramelized Pear Filling. Continue with remaining cake layers and pear filling, ending with a layer of cake on top. Refrigerate 1-2 hours to let the filling firm up.

Spread Chocolate Glaze over the top and sides of the cake. Refrigerate for 30 minutes or overnight.

Cut into slices and serve. Serves 10-12.

CREAM PUFFS *with* CARAMELIZED PEAR FILLING *and* CHOCOLATE GLAZE

The Caramelized Pear Filling and the Chocolate Glaze make a rich combination, so you will want to make your cream puffs small.

◆◆◆

1 recipe Chocolate Glaze
 (recipe follows)
1 recipe Caramelized Pear Filling
 (recipe follows)

1/2 cup water
1/4 cup butter
1/2 cup flour
1/8 teaspoon salt
2 large eggs

▲▲▲▲

Preheat oven to 400°.

Heat the butter and water in a small saucepan until the butter is melted. Remove from the heat. Add the flour and salt. Return to medium heat and cook, stirring constantly, until the mixture is smooth and forms a ball, pulling away from the sides of the pan. Continue cooking 2 minutes to dry out the dough. Remove from the heat and cool slightly. Add the eggs, one at a time, beating until the mixture is smooth before adding another.

Place small, walnut-sized mounds 2″ apart on an ungreased cookie sheet that has been sprinkled with water. Bake in a preheated oven 15-20 minutes. Makes 18-20 small puffs.

To assemble: Cut the top third off the Cream Puff Shells, reserving the tops. Scoop out any soft interiors and discard. Fill each Cream Puff Shell with 2-3 tablespoons of the Caramelized Pear Filling. Place the tops back on the Cream Puff Shells and drizzle each puff with the Chocolate Glaze. Serves 8-10.

◆

CARAMELIZED PEAR FILLING

6 tablespoons butter
2 pounds ripe pears
1 tablespoon gelatin
1 tablespoon pear brandy*
2 tablespoons water*
2/3 cup sugar

▲▲▲▲

Melt the butter in a heavy-bottomed skillet. Add the pears and cook, stirring occasionally, until they are softened, 15-20 minutes. When softened, transfer to the work bowl of a food processor. Using the metal blade, process until the pear mixture is smooth.

Mix together the water and pear brandy. Dissolve the gelatin in the mixture.

Heat the sugar in a small skillet until it turns a deep golden brown. With the processor running, carefully pour the hot sugar into the pear mixture. Scrape down the sides of the work bowl to loosen any bits of sugar.

Add the dissolved gelatin and process to combine gelatin and bits of hardened sugar.

Transfer to a bowl and set aside to cool. When cool, refrigerate until firm, 2-3 hours. (This will hold for up to two weeks when sealed tightly and refrigerated.) Makes 2 cups.

*You may use 3 tablespoons dessert wine for the water and pear brandy, or use 3 tablespoons water.

◆

CHOCOLATE GLAZE

4 ounces bittersweet chocolate
1/4 cup butter

▲▲▲▲

Melt the butter and chocolate together. Set aside to drizzle over the the finished puffs.

FILBERT ROULADE *with* COFFEE CREAM FILLING

If you love coffee and filberts, you are sure to love this recipe!

◆◆◆

1 recipe Coffee Cream (recipe follows)
1 15½" × 10½" × 1" jelly roll pan

◆

CAKE

6 large eggs, separated
²/₃ cup sugar
1 teaspoon instant coffee powder
  (not granules)
½ teaspoon baking powder
²/₃ cup finely ground toasted filberts
2 teaspoons filbert liqueur
2 teaspoons coffee liqueur
2 teaspoons water

▲▲▲▲

Preheat the oven to 400°.

Oil and line a baking sheet with parchment or waxed paper. Butter and flour the paper.

Beat the egg yolks, sugar, coffee powder, and baking powder until the mixture is thick and forms ribbons when the beater is lifted.

Beat the egg whites until stiff but not dry. Sprinkle the ground nuts over the egg whites. Pour the yolk mixture over the egg white-nuts mixture and gently fold to combine.

Pour batter into the prepared pan and bake 20-25 minutes, until a toothpick inserted in the center comes out clean and the cake is brown.

Invert onto a powdered sugar dusted cotton towel. Remove the baking paper and roll up, starting with the short edge. Set on a rack to cool.

◆

COFFEE CREAM FILLING

1 package gelatin
3 tablespoons cold water
¼ cup instant coffee powder
  (not granules)
½ cup boiling water
2 eggs
⅓ cup sugar
1 cup whipping cream

▲▲▲▲

Soften the gelatin in the cold water.

Dissolve the coffee powder in the boiling water. Add the softened gelatin to the hot coffee and stir to combine. Make sure the gelatin is completely dissolved; heat gently if necessary to dissolve completely. Set aside to cool.

Combine the eggs and sugar in the top of a double boiler, mixing well. Place over simmering water and beat until the mixture is thick and is 140°. Set aside to cool. When cool, combine the cooled coffee and egg mixtures.

Whip the cream and fold into the coffee mixture. Refrigerate 15 minutes until firm enough to work with.

To assemble: Set aside 1½ cups Coffee Cream. Combine 2 teaspoons each filbert liqueur, coffee liqueur, and water.

Unroll the cooled cake and brush with the liqueur and water mixture. Spread remaining Coffee Cream over the unrolled cake.

Gently re-roll the cake and refrigerate to let the filling set up. After the roll has set 15 minutes, remove from the refrigerator and frost with the reserved 1½ cups coffee cream. Refrigerate one hour or overnight. Serves 10.

STEAMBOAT INN'S FRUIT PIES

Alice Bellior, our baker, works two full days a week just to keep up with the cinnamon rolls and pies we serve during our summer season. As you can see from the suggestions below, the fruit combinations are endless. We have included the recipe for our most often requested pie—Raspberry Rhubarb.

◆◆◆

1 recipe Crust
   (recipe follows)
1 recipe Raspberry-Rhubarb Pie Filling
   (recipe follows)

◆

CRUST

2 cups flour
1 teaspoon salt
$^2/_3$ cup cold butter or shortening
3-4 tablespoons ice water

▲▲▲▲

Combine the flour and salt. Cut in the butter until it resembles coarse meal. Add the water, one tablespoon at a time, mixing with a fork until the dough holds together. Form into a ball; then divide in half. Wrap half the dough in plastic wrap and set aside.

Roll out the remaining dough on a lightly floured board until the circle of dough is $1^1/_4$" wider than a 9-10"" pie plate. Fold the pastry in half and place in an ungreased pie plate. Unfold, with the excess draped over the edge of the pie plate.

Fill the pie shell with the desired filling and dot with 2 tablespoons butter or margarine.

Roll out the remaining dough on a lightly floured board into an 11" circle. Fold dough in half. With a sharp knife cut several slits near the center seam to allow steam to escape.

Lay the top crust over the filling with the fold at the center of the pie. Unfold and trim the edge of the crust to within $^1/_2$" of the top of the pie plate. Fold the overhang over and crimp the top and bottom crusts together. Brush the top of the pie with milk or a beaten egg, and bake at 400° 45-60 minutes.

◆

RASPBERRY-RHUBARB PIE FILLING

3 cups $^1/_2$" rhubarb slices, fresh or frozen
1 cup raspberries, fresh or frozen
$^2/_3$-$^3/_4$ cups sugar
   (amount depends on berry sweetness)
3 tablespoons flour
$^1/_4$ teaspoon nutmeg
dash of salt

▲▲▲▲

Combine the ingredients, mixing well. This makes enough filling for a 9-10" pie.

Other fruit combinations: Plum-Apple, Apple-Blueberry, Apple-Blackberry, Cherry-Apple, Strawberry-Rhubarb, Blackberry-Raspberry, Peach-Blueberry, Peach-Raspberry.

BROILED PEAR *with* LIME SAUCE

This light and tangy dessert is an especially nice finish to a spicy meal.

◆◆◆

1 recipe Lime Sauce (recipe follows)

◆

BROILED PEARS

3 firm, ripe pears
1 tablespoon sugar
6 slices fresh lime
1 teaspoon coffee granules

▲▲▲▲

Preheat the broiler.

Cut the pears in half and core. Cut slits in the pear every $1/8$ inch as if you were going to slice it, but only go $1/4$ inch deep.

Place the pear halves on a baking pan and sprinkle with the sugar and coffee granules. Broil 3-5 minutes, until the pears are heated through and the sugar has started to caramelize.

◆

LIME SAUCE

$1/4$ cup sugar
3 tablespoons light Karo Syrup®
1 tablespoon honey
1 tablespoon cornstarch
1 cup champagne
3 tablespoons butter
$1/2$ teaspoon lime zest
3 tablespoons fresh lime juice

▲▲▲▲

Combine the sugar, Karo Syrup®, honey, cornstarch, and champagne in a nonreactive saucepan. Simmer until the mixture is thickened and no longer opaque.

Stir in the butter, lime zest, and juice. Remove from the heat and set aside.

To assemble: Pour a pool of Lime Sauce on each of 6 serving dishes. Top with a Broiled Pear half and garnish with a slice of fresh lime. Serves 6.

GINGER SORBET

A creamy and richly flavored sorbet, one that makes an ideal light dessert.

◆◆◆

$1^1/2$ cups sugar
2 tablespoons minced fresh ginger root
2 teaspoons lemon zest
4 cups water
2 cups nonfat vanilla yogurt

▲▲▲▲

Combine the first three ingredients in the bowl of a food processor and process until the ginger and zest are very fine.

Transfer the ginger mixture to a 2-quart saucepan. Add the water. Boil, uncovered, over medium heat 10 minutes. Remove from the heat and cool. When the mixture is cool, fold in the yogurt. Freeze in an ice cream maker, following the manufacturer's instructions. Makes 7 cups, serving 8-10.

APPLE CINNAMON TORTE

This dessert is best served the day it is made. Homemade vanilla ice cream topped with freshly grated nutmeg is a wonderful accompaniment.

◆◆◆

1 11" tart pan with removable bottom, lightly buttered

1 recipe Crust (recipe follows)

1 recipe Topping (recipe follows)

◆

CRUST

1 cup flour
$\frac{1}{2}$ cup sugar
$\frac{1}{4}$ teaspoon nutmeg
$\frac{1}{4}$ cup butter, cut in chunks
1 egg, lightly beaten

▲▲▲▲

Using a food processor, mix the flour, sugar, and nutmeg. Add the butter and process until combined. Add the egg and process until the mixture resembles coarse meal.

Pour into the buttered tart shell. Press the crust onto the sides of the pan and over the bottom.

Preheat oven to 350°.

◆

APPLES

5 large Granny Smith apples, (about $2\frac{1}{2}$ pounds) peeled and cored

▲▲▲▲

Cut $2\frac{1}{2}$ of the apples into small chunks. Scatter these over the crust. Thinly slice the remaining $2\frac{1}{2}$ apples and arrange these on top of the chopped apple.

Bake 35 minutes. Pour the topping over the apples and bake an additional 15-20 minutes, until set. Serve warm or at room temperature. Serves 8-10.

◆

TOPPING

3 eggs
7 tablespoons butter, melted
7 tablespoons sugar
1 tablespoon cinnamon
$\frac{1}{4}$ teaspoon nutmeg

▲▲▲▲

While the torte is baking, combine all of the ingredients, mixing well.

ORANGE WALNUT CAKE
with ORANGE SYRUP

This light but firm cake packs well for a picnic. Though it doesn't need frosting, leftover syrup can be mixed with whipped cream and used as a garnish.

◆◆◆

1 10″ Bundt pan, buttered and floured

1 cup butter, room temperature
1³/₄ cup sugar
4 teaspoons finely minced orange zest
5 eggs
1¹/₄ cups buttermilk
1 teaspoon baking soda
3¹/₂ cups flour
1¹/₄ cups coarsely chopped walnuts

1 recipe Orange Syrup (recipe follows)
sweetened whipped cream (optional)

▲▲▲▲

Preheat oven to 350°.
   Cream the butter and sugar. Add the minced zest. Add the eggs, one at a time.
   Combine the buttermilk and baking soda.
   Alternately add the buttermilk mixture and the flour to the cake batter. Fold in the chopped nuts. Pour into the prepared pan and bake 40-50 minutes.

Remove the cake from the oven and let set 5 minutes. Brush the top of the cake with the Orange Syrup. Unmold the cake onto a cooling rack and place the rack on a baking sheet. Brush the cake on the bottom and sides with the Orange Syrup. Over the next 30-40 minutes, brush the entire cake several times with the Orange Syrup. Serve warm or at room temperature. Serves 12-16.

◆

ORANGE SYRUP

¹/₂ cup fresh-squeezed orange juice
³/₄ cup sugar
1 teaspoon finely minced orange zest

▲▲▲▲

Combine the ingredients in a small, non-reactive saucepan. Heat over medium heat until the sugar has dissolved and the mixture is clear. Remove from the heat. Store in an air-tight container in the refrigerator. The syrup will hold for several months. Bring to room temperature before using.

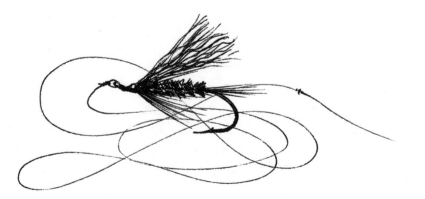

DRIED PEAR *and* WALNUT BISCOTTI

These dense, slightly sweet cookies will store for several days if kept in an airtight container.

◆◆◆

3 eggs
1 cup sugar
$\frac{1}{2}$ cup dried snipped pears
1 cup chopped walnuts
$\frac{1}{4}$ teaspoon walnut flavoring
$3\frac{1}{2}$ cups white flour
$\frac{1}{3}$ cup corn flour
$1\frac{1}{2}$ teaspoons baking powder

▲▲▲▲

Preheat the oven to 350°.

Beat the eggs with the sugar until thickened and pale yellow.

Fold the melted butter into the batter. Fold in the pears, nuts, and walnut flavoring.

Combine the flours and baking powder. Fold the flour mixture into the egg mixture a fourth at a time (the dough will be very thick). When all is incorporated, divide the dough in half. Form each half into a cylinder $1\frac{1}{2}$" in diameter and 8-10" long. Place on a parchment-covered baking sheet and bake 15-20 minutes, until golden. Remove from the oven and cut into $\frac{1}{2}$" slices. Place the cut slices on the baking sheet. Bake an additional 8-10 minutes, until the slices no longer look wet in the middle and are crisp. Makes 30-36 cookies.

ALMOND BUTTER BARS

This chewy bar not only packs well in a picnic basket but it is as easy to prepare as it is to eat!

◆◆◆

1 8" × 8" baking pan, buttered

$\frac{1}{4}$ cup butter
$\frac{1}{3}$ cup almond butter
$\frac{1}{2}$ cup packed brown sugar
2 eggs
$\frac{1}{2}$ teaspoon vanilla extract
$\frac{1}{4}$ teaspoon almond extract
$\frac{1}{8}$ teaspoon salt
$\frac{2}{3}$ cup flour
$\frac{1}{2}$ teaspoon baking powder
$\frac{1}{3}$ cup semi-sweet chocolate chips
$\frac{1}{4}$ cup sliced almonds

▲▲▲▲

Preheat oven to 350°.

Cream the butters and sugar. Beat in the eggs. Add the extracts.

Combine the salt, flour, and baking powder. Add to the butter mixture. Fold in the chocolate chips. Pour into the prepared pan and top with the sliced almonds. Bake 20-25 minutes. Cool before cutting. Makes about 20 small bar cookies.

BUTTERMILK POPPY SEED CAKE

Though we have included a Honey Lemon Glaze, this light cake really needs no frosting and, when made with fructose, it is suitable for a diabetic diet.

♦♦♦

1 cup buttermilk
1/3 cup poppy seeds
2 1/2 cups flour
1 teaspoon baking powder
1/4 teaspoon salt
1 cup butter or margarine,
    room temperature
1 1/2 cups sugar or 1 cup fructose
    (natural fruit sugar)
4 eggs, separated
2 teaspoons vanilla
1 teaspoon lemon zest, finely minced
1/2 teaspoon baking soda

1 recipe Honey-Lemon Glaze
    (recipe follows)

▲▲▲▲

Preheat oven to 350°.
    Butter and flour a bundt pan.
    Combine the buttermilk and poppy seeds. Let set for 20 minutes.
    Sift the flour, baking powder, and salt.

Cream the butter. Add the sugar. Beat in the egg yolks one at a time. Add the vanilla and lemon zest. Stir the baking soda into the poppy seed mixture.
    Add half the flour mixture to the creamed butter. Follow with half of the poppy seed-buttermilk mixture. Continue with the rest of the flour and poppy seed-buttermilk mixture.
    Beat the egg whites until stiff but not dry. Stir a quarter of the whites into the batter to lighten it. Gently fold in the remaining whites. Pour into the prepared bundt pan. Bake 35-40 minutes.
    Remove from the oven and let set in the pan 10 minutes. Remove from the pan and set on a rack to cool. (This cake freezes well.) When cool, pour glaze over cake. Serves 16.

♦

HONEY-LEMON GLAZE

1 cup sifted powdered sugar
1/2 teaspoon minced lemon zest
1 tablespoon honey
1 tablespoon lemon juice

▲▲▲▲

Combine all ingredients, mixing well.

Wine
&
Menus

The Pinot Family Comes to Dinner

by Stephen J. Cary and David J. Anderson

In THYME AND THE RIVER, we outlined food and wine pairings for the most popular grape varieties. For THYME & THE RIVER TOO, we are focusing on a single family of grapes, the Pinots.

Pinot Noir is the red grape of the Burgundy district in France. Historically, it has not prospered in many other sites around the globe. In the last twenty-five years, however, that has changed. By restricting themselves to very specific cool climatic sites, viticulturists are now succeeding in growing excellent Pinots in selected areas around the globe. The Yarra Valley in Australia, the Martinborough District in New Zealand, the Carneros District, Russian River Valley, south coast areas of California, and certainly the western valleys of Oregon are now producing beautiful Pinot family wines.

Pinot Noir is indigenous to Burgundy. The earliest writings indicate that it was cultivated there before the Romans arrived more than two thousand years ago. Since 1395, by decree of the Duke of Burgundy, it has been the only red variety legally planted in their finest vineyards.

The Pinot family is relatively unstable genetically. Growers must contend with field mutations even in young vineyards. This propensity for evolutionary change, in fact, has brought about the development of two white Pinot family members, Pinot Blanc and Pinot Gris.

Since the 1400s, these two varieties have been kept separate and propagated for the white wines they produce.

Some wines are very limited in the number of dishes they will successfully complement. The Pinot family, on the other hand, is amazingly successful across a huge range of dishes, including diverse ethnic, style, and ingredient preparations. Faced with the old desert island theoretical question, they are the wines we would choose.

The reason Pinots work so well with so many dishes is because they do not overwhelm the food. The wines are both subtle and elegant, blending into the meal like two clear streams flowing together, neither clouding the other. At the same time, these wines maintain the ability to cleanse the palate, to keep one's mouth fresh to enjoy the entire meal. It is this rare ability to maintain their own identity without dominating foods that makes the Pinots so remarkable. With our cuisine becoming ever more complex and graceful, they are most often the wines of choice.

Pinot Gris is a delightful, fruity, dry white wine that sometimes has a hint of salmon color from the grapes. We see it from Alsace, Italy, (Pinot Grigio), and now Oregon. It was meant for fish dishes that accentuate light, delicate qualities. In THYME & THE RIVER TOO, we suggest pouring it with scallops, oysters, crab, shrimp, smoked trout, smoked salmon, and non-meat pasta dishes. The only time a fish preparation does not work well with Pinot Gris is when it is grilled.

Pinot Blanc is a bit weightier, more serious white wine than Pinot Gris. It is grown in the Pinot Gris areas, plus California and some other sites around the globe. Pinot Gris often has an apple-like nose, but Pinot Blanc smells more of melons. The color is most often in the straw tones. It does well with the same courses as Pinot Gris but also matches richer foods, such as Poached Eggs on Smoked Salmon Polenta with Sun-Dried Tomatoes, Roasted Chicken, Spaghetti Squash Patties with Saffron Sauce, Turkey and Dried Apple Sausage, and pasta dishes with chicken or turkey.

Pinot Noir ranges from delicate light red to full-bodied versions, depending on origin, producer, and vintage. In its lighter style, it makes a great picnic wine with smoked meats, grilled fowl, spicy mushroom dishes, and pâtés. In these cases, serve slightly chilled to make the wine more refreshing. Full-bodied Pinots are the perfect complement to Grilled Salmon, Roasted Pork, Peppered Duck Breast, Spicy Lamb, and Stuffed Flank Steak.

The number of matches between food and Pinot appears endless. The only combinations we tend to avoid are noticeably sweet entrées or those with a pronounced bitterness. And there are times when even that rule of thumb should be ignored. For instance, the best wine to put with raspberry and chocolate desserts is a full-bodied Pinot Noir!

◆

FRESH FRUIT PLATE

*POACHED EGGS on SMOKED SALMON POLENTA
with SUN-DRIED TOMATO BUTTER SAUCE*

TURKEY and DRIED APPLE SAUSAGE

BROCCOLI with SMOKED ALMONDS

CRANBERRY-APPLE STRUDEL

◆

LEMON-POPPY SEED MUFFINS

SALMON QUENELLES with TARRAGON SAUCE

CRISP BACON

STEAMED ASPARAGUS

BROILED PEAR with LIME SAUCE

◆

APRICOT-PECAN SCONES

*SPINACH ROULADE with CHICKEN FILLING
and SABAYON SAUCE*

CARROT ALMOND SALAD*

GARNISH of RED APPLE and KIWI

*TOASTED NUT LACE COOKIE CUP
with VANILLA ICE CREAM and FRESH BERRIES*

*Recipe may be found in *Thyme and the River.*

LUNCH MENUS

◆

SHRIMP, BROCCOLI and CORN GÂTEAU
with RED PEPPER-BASIL SAUCE

FRESH FRUIT PLATE

ROASTED GARLIC and ROSEMARY BREAD

◆

TURKEY NECTARINE SALAD

CROISSANTS

◆

CHICKEN and BLACK BEAN CHILI

MIXED GREEN SALAD

CORNMEAL MUFFINS

◆

FLANK STEAK and BAVARIAN BLUE CHEESE SANDWICH

CARROT-THYME SOUP

FRESH PEARS

◆

BROCCOLI NOODLE SALAD

SMOKED TROUT and PASTA SALAD

"PIZZA" PICNIC BREAD

PECAN and FRESH GINGER TART
with CORNMEAL CRUST

◆

SMOKED SALMON POTATO SALAD

SPICY CUCUMBERS

PEANUT DIP with FRESH VEGETABLES

CURRIED LENTIL PÂTÉ

DUCK and CHICKEN PÂTÉ

FRENCH BREAD

CHOCOLATE FILBERT TORTE

◆

GRILLED CHICKEN BREASTS
with ROASTED GARLIC MAYONNAISE

ORZO and FETA SALAD

MUSHROOM-FETA PICNIC BREAD

MIDDLE EASTERN GARBANZO BEANS

BUTTERMILK POPPY SEED CAKE

DINNER MENUS

◆

**SPINACH SALAD
with PEARS and PEPPER ALMONDS**

**PEPPERED DUCK BREAST
with MARIONBERRY CATSUP**

WILD RICE PANCAKES

BEET GREENS and MUSHROOMS

ROASTED GARLIC and ROSEMARY BREAD

RASPBERRY TART

◆

GREEN SALAD with NAPA CABBAGE

OVEN ROASTED CHICKEN

PORCINI MUSHROOM RISOTTO

**STIR FRY of BROCCOLI, CORN,
RED PEPPER, and ONION**

CRISP FRENCH BREAD

**CREAM PUFFS with CARAMELIZED PEAR FILLING
and CHOCOLATE GLAZE**

◆

MIXED GREEN SALAD

SCALLOPS in ONION-WINE SAUCE

ANGEL HAIR PASTA

SESAME CORN

**TOASTED COCONUT CAKE
with TOASTED COCONUT-PECAN FILLING**

Although the majority of our recipes utilize fresh and local ingredients, we felt it would be helpful to offer an explanation for a few specialty items. Many large grocery stores now carry international foods on their specialty aisle, and we have found our local grocers more than cooperative in ordering ingredients we have had difficulty finding. Many of our requested items are now stocked because they have sold so well!

APRICOT MUSTARD:

> 7 ounces dried apricots
> 4 tablespoons Dijon mustard
> boiling water

Cover the apricots with boiling water; then cover tightly and set aside until the apricots are soft and plumped. Drain.

Puree apricots and mustard until smooth. Do not worry if there are some small bits of apricot in the mustard. Refrigerate until ready to use. Makes 1 cup.

BALSAMIC VINEGAR: A sweet-sour, wine-based Italian vinegar that has undergone long aging in a variety of wooden barrels—each a different wood. It is now generally available in most large grocery stores and may be used in marinades or dressings, or just splashed on freshly steamed vegetables.

BARBECUE SMOKING: This method will impart a wonderful flavor to your meat and is an easy smoking alternative for those who do not have access to a smoker.

> 3/4 cup smoking chips
> 2 cups water

Soak the smoking chips in the water for half an hour. While the chips are soaking, prepare the barbecue.

Just as the coals have started to turn gray, sprinkle the chips over the coals and add the fish, chicken, or meat you are going to smoke. Cover the barbecue and shut all the air drafts. Check and turn the meat frequently until it is cooked through. Do not be concerned if it turns dark on the outside.

CHILI GARLIC SAUCE: This is a very spicy chili sauce. We often use this in place of dried chilies as it provides a fuller flavor.

CHIMI CHURRI SAUCE: Jorge Graziosi, our good Argentine friend who visits the Inn each fall, introduced us to this sauce. It is found on the table in most Argentine restaurants where it is used to flavor meat. We use it in our vegetarian burgers, to baste meat while barbecuing, and in marinades.

> 1/4 cup minced onion
> 1 teaspoon minced fresh garlic
> 2 tablespoons dried leaf oregano
> 1 tablespoon crushed red chilies
> 2 tablespoons rock salt
> 1/4 teaspoon paprika
> dash of cayenne
> 1 cup very hot water

Combine all ingredients, mixing well. Stores indefinitely when refrigerated. Makes 1 cup.

EGGS: In our recipes, we always use large eggs unless otherwise stated.

FILBERT PASTE:

    10 ounces (about 2 cups) toasted filberts
    ³/₄ cup sugar
    2 tablespoons filbert liqueur

Process the toasted nuts in the work bowl of a food processor until coarsely chopped. Add the sugar and grind as fine as possible. Add the liqueur and process with one or two on-off turns.

You should have a soft, crumbly mixture. Use immediately or seal airtight and refrigerate. Makes 12 ounces of paste, enough for two Chocolate Filbert Tortes (recipe page 114).

GINGER, CRYSTALLIZED: Ginger that has been sliced, dried, and sugared. It is now carried by most large grocery stores.

GINGER, FRESH: Fresh ginger is available in the produce sections of most large grocery stores. It has a short shelf life when just left in a bag in the refrigerator.

To store for a longer time, peel and place in a nonreactive container. Cover with dry sherry; then cover tightly and refrigerate. It holds indefinitely. The "gingered sherry" is a great addition to soups and stir fries.

GINGER, PICKLED: When sliced into thin strips and preserved in red brine, ginger can be stored indefinitely under refrigeration. Pickled ginger has a crisp, ginger flavor. This is available in most large grocery stores.

HERBS: When fresh herbs are not available, we use crushed, rather than powdered. If powdered herbs are used, we decrease the amounts called for.

HOT CHILI OIL: A hot, spicy oil made from infusing spicy red peppers into either sesame or vegetable oil. It may also be found under the names: "chili oil," "hot pepper oil," or "red oil." To assure freshness, purchase it in small jars.

PICO PICA®: This is one of many Mexican-style hot sauces that are available. We have not explored the market in depth but have found Pico Pica® to lend a hearty spiciness without being harsh.

PHYLLO (FILO or FILLO): This is a paper-thin pastry that is used to encase fillings for appetizers, entrées, and desserts. Phyllo is available fresh or frozen from delis or some grocery stores. If purchased frozen, let thaw in the refrigerator for two days before using. Phyllo will dry out rapidly if left exposed, so keep the dough covered with a towel when working with it.

RED PEPPERS, ROASTED: Roasted red peppers are now available on the grocery shelves, or you can roast you own.

To roast over an open flame: Skewer a whole pepper on a large fork and roast over a gas flame, turning frequently, until blackened all over. Transfer to a paper bag, close the bag, and let the peppers steam 20 to 25 minutes. Remove from the bag and peel off the skin. Open up and remove the seeds.

To roast in the oven: Preheat the broiler. Cut the peppers in half and seed. Place skin-side-up on a roasting pan and broil until the skin has blackened. Transfer to a paper bag and let steam 20 minutes. Remove from the bag and peel off the skin.

Refrigerate any unused peppers in an airtight container. You can also freeze them.

REDUCE/REDUCTION: This is a process of condensing liquid over high heat to intensify flavor. Keep in mind most commercial stocks are salted and reducing them will heighten the salt flavor in your dish.

RICE VINEGAR: A Japanese vinegar, white-to-golden in color, that is less harsh and more full-flavored than most distilled vinegars.

You will also see a seasoned rice vinegar on the grocery shelf; this generally has sugar added to it.

RICE WINE (AJI MIRIN): A sweetened Japanese cooking wine. Sake may be used as a substitute.

ROASTED GARLIC or SHALLOTS:

1 head garlic
2 tablespoons oil
$1/4$-$1/2$ cup water

Preheat oven to 375°.

Take a thin slice off the top of the head of garlic. Rub the head with 1 tablespoon of the oil and place in a small bread pan. Place $1/4$ to $1/2$ cup water and the remaining tablespoon of oil in the pan. Cover with foil.

Bake in preheated oven 1 to $1 1/2$ hours, until the garlic is soft and easily slips out of the skin. Cool. Cover and refrigerate until ready to use.

SEAWEED, DRIED (or YAKISUSHI-NORI): These are flat sheets, approximately 8″ by 8″, of dried seaweed, which are used in making rolled sushi.

SNIPPED: We have coined this kitchen term as we use scissors to cut up (snip) ingredients that are difficult to cut with a knife.

Try using scissors instead of a pizza wheel to cut a pizza sometime!

STOCKS: Generally, we use hearty, home-made, unsalted stocks. Be very careful when reducing commercial "broths" as they may be very salty, and the salt intensifies as the broth reduces. *Swansons®* is now offering a lightly salted broth, and there may be others available in your area.

SUN-DRIED TOMATOES: When these were first on the grocery shelves, they were only available in oil pack. You can now find them packed dry. The tomatoes called for in our recipes are the dry-pack version. They have less calories and do not add additional oil to a recipe.

TOASTING NUTS: We always ask for toasted nuts in our recipes. Toasting the nuts freshens their flavor. In some instances, toasting produces a completely different, and much more interesting, flavor.

To toast the nuts, preheat an oven to 375°. Spread the nuts in a single layer on a baking sheet. Bake until golden. This can take anywhere from 10 to 20 minutes, depending on the nut itself or the moisture content of the nut. Check the nuts frequently as they will burn very easily.

If you are toasting filberts, remove them from the oven and transfer to a kitchen towel. Rub them in the towel to remove as much of the skin as possible.

THYME & THE RIVER TOO is no exception to the fact that the name or names on the cover of a book can never reflect all of the people responsible for the final product. Dan Callaghan's scenic photographs grace the pages of this book as they did THYME AND THE RIVER. Not only is Dan a fine photographer but a loyal friend and supporter, always ready with an encouraging word and more than willing to respond to our requests for assistance. The food photographs are the work of John Rizzo. John, his assistant Matt Cooper, and food stylist Lori McKean have become members of our extended Steamboat family. We thoroughly enjoyed the days they spent on the river photographing our recipes. Their unfailing good humor, despite the spring rain showers, and willingness to spend the time to get the photograph "just right" made their participation in the project fun for us.

The artwork in this volume is that of river resident David Hall. David has been a strong supporter of the river and the Inn for many years. We feel fortunate he was able to take time out from his busy schedule to do this book. Thanks, David—we appreciate you and the thought you put into this project.

We would like to give special thanks to Trey Combs for sharing his interest in the North Umpqua and his research on the fly patterns and their originators.

Enough cannot be said about the wonderful staff we have at the Inn. They have exhibited great patience with our "commandeering" the Inn's small kitchen and are always willing to offer critiques of our experiments—even when it is the tenth version of the same recipe! As you will see in reading the book, several of our staff have contributed recipes to this volume.

In the same vein, we have to offer thanks to this year's construction crew. We fed them many multicourse lunches with some strange food combinations, all of which they accepted with a willing palate. One could say they were extremely cooperative when we spent two weeks on desserts alone!

Once again, our dear friends, Stephen Cary (winemaker) and David Anderson (general manager) from Yamhill Valley Vineyards, responded to our request for an article on wine. Special thanks to both Stephen and David, not only for their wine knowledge, but, most importantly, for their wonderful friendship.

As she did with our first book, Shelley Bedell-Stiles lent her keen eye and attention to detail in editing our work. Thank you, Shelley. We look forward to working with you again one day. Our thanks, once again, to Jean Andrews for her editorial skills. Jean spent many long hours to assure the book was consistent in its format and readability. We appreciate you always being available to answer even the smallest question.

As always, our thanks and love to Keith and Jim, our husbands.

Patricia Lee and Sharon Van Loan